PRAISE FOR B2B CUSTOMER EXPERIENCE

'While much has been written about customer experience in the consumer space, the business-to-business sector is typically neglected. The focus on B2B is what makes this book a compelling read. Nick and Paul Hague's vast experience has been detailed in five easily digestible sections that hold the reader's hand from "Why bother?" through to developing strategies and implementation of CX. The case studies where clients share their experiences in their own words help bring the authors' concepts to life.' **Shep Hyken, customer service and experience expert and** *New York Times* **bestselling author of** *The Amazement Revolution*

'Nick and Paul Hague have done an extraordinary job of capturing every aspect of how to create and maintain world-class B2B customer service for any industry or organization, from healthcare to manufacturing to airlines, and even to help entrepreneurs figure out how to compete with the big guys. I consider myself an expert on customer service after my 42 years with Hilton Hotels, Marriott International and my final role of running Walt Disney World Operations for 10 years, but I can honestly say I learned some new ways to think about going from average to good, to great, to greater with customer service. Keep this book on your desk as your go-to resource for creating magic for your customers.' **Lee Cockerell, former Executive Vice President of Operations, Walt Disney World Resort,** *Creating Disney Magic* **podcast host and author of four bestsellers on leadership, management and customer service**

'One thing that all businesses and consumers have in common is that they are on the receiving end of customer experiences on a daily basis. While consumer-facing organizations have been consciously aware of this fact for many years, organizations that predominantly provide products and services to other businesses, rather than to consumers directly, have been much slower to catch on. Defining, delivering and managing the customer experience in a B2B environment is becoming ever more critical in a business world that continues to be challenged and disrupted from many fronts.

'Nick and Paul Hague not only recognize this, they have pulled together a piece of work that will help any organization understand how to turn the words "customer experience" into a tangible reality – a reality that leads to improved customer perception AND financial performance. The authors brilliantly provide the building blocks that turn the science of customer experience into something you will be able to practically adopt and deploy. *B2B Customer Experience* is a hugely valuable read for anyone who has an aspiration to achieve sustainable growth.' **Ian Golding, CCXP, global customer experience specialist and author of *Customer What?***

'Nick and Paul Hague have put together one of the best books looking at the whole of customer experience I have seen to date. Tying together employee metrics and a collection of customer metrics such as Customer Effort Score, customer satisfaction, Net Value Score, and Net Promoter Score®, they have specific suggestions for how to think about, measure and benchmark the customer experience within a business context. This is an excellent view of how to think about and move forward with CX in your business.' **Roy Atkinson, CX expert and Principal, Clifton Butterfield, LLC**

'Nick and Paul Hague do a brilliant job of tackling a topic that many have written off as impossible – how to deliver a great B2B customer experience. If you're in a B2B business and have customers who you want to delight, this book is a must-read. The Hagues masterfully take the reader through each of the foundational elements that are critical to designing and delivering a great customer experience in an easy-to-understand approach that is supported by customer stories and case studies, making this book a practical guide for your successful B2B customer experience transformation.' **Annette Franz, CCXP, founder and CEO, CX Journey Inc**

'Too many of the books that are written about customer experience are dominated by insights and stories from B2C companies and markets. Therefore, it's refreshing to find a book that has been written with B2B companies and markets in mind. This is a really useful guide that will help B2B executives understand and apply the fundamental elements of what it takes to deliver a great customer experience.' **Adrian Swinscoe, adviser and bestselling author of *How to Wow: 68 effortless ways to make every customer experience amazing***

'There are more B2B companies than B2C companies in the world. Every B2B company needs to be an experience-led business. This book will help you become one.' **Blake Morgan, customer experience futurist and author of _More Is More_**

'Become a customer journey addict. Learn how to do it with practical guidance from Nick and Paul Hague, the experts who know it all but still get excited about every project.' **Antoine Philippe, Head of Marketing, Etex**

'An essential guide to customer experience, one of the biggest trends shaping the future of business. This is an intelligent, practical and wise collection of advice from leading sources, experts and thinkers, supported by real company experiences and field data.' **Gordon Hay, Operations Director, Brenntag**

'On the surface, delivering service excellence may seem easy. When you deep dive, delivering a world-class customer experience isn't easy at all. This well-researched, well-written and compelling book gives the reader the insights needed and the framework required to implement a customer experience strategy that will deliver real benefit to both the business and its clients.' **Donna Whitbrook, Corporate Associate, First Impressions Training Ltd**

'A clearly written, relevant book that goes beyond the theory and offers practical examples. As a contributor, it was great to read that we are all still on the journey: no one is "done" yet – it is comforting to know we're all in a similar situation.' **Carol Sheppard, Customer Experience Manager, Molson Coors**

B2B
Customer
Experience

B2B Customer Experience

A practical guide to delivering exceptional CX

Nick Hague and Paul Hague

KoganPage

Publisher's note

Every possible effort has been made to ensure that the information contained in this book is accurate at the time of going to press, and the publisher and authors cannot accept responsibility for any errors or omissions, however caused. No responsibility for loss or damage occasioned to any person acting, or refraining from action, as a result of the material in this publication can be accepted by the editor, the publisher or the authors.

First published in Great Britain and the United States in 2018 by Kogan Page Limited

2nd Floor, 45 Gee Street	c/o Martin P Hill Consulting	4737/23 Ansari Road
London	122 W 27th St, 10th Floor	Daryaganj
EC1V 3RS	New York NY 10001	New Delhi 110002
United Kingdom	USA	India
www.koganpage.com		

© Nick Hague and Paul Hague, 2018

The right of Nick Hague and Paul Hague to be identified as the authors of this work has been asserted by them in accordance with the Copyright, Designs and Patents Act 1988.

ISBN   978 0 7494 8185 8
E-ISBN 978 0 7494 8186 5

British Library Cataloguing-in-Publication Data

A CIP record for this book is available from the British Library.

Library of Congress Cataloging-in-Publication Data

Names: Hague, Nick, 1974- author. | Hague, Paul N., author.
Title: B2B customer experience : a practical guide to delivering exceptional CX / Nick Hague and Paul Hague.
Description: 1st Edition. | New York, NY : Kogan Page Ltd, [2018] | Includes bibliographical references and index.
Identifiers: LCCN 2018015738 (print) | LCCN 2018021537 (ebook) | ISBN 9780749481865 (ebook) | ISBN 9780749481858 (pbk.)
Subjects: LCSH: Customer relations. | Customer loyalty.
Classification: LCC HF5415.5 (ebook) | LCC HF5415.5 .H244 2018 (print) | DDC 658.8/12–dc23

Typeset by Integra Software Services, Pondicherry
Print production managed by Jellyfish
Printed and bound by CPI Group (UK) Ltd, Croydon, CR0 4YY

CONTENTS

PREFACE

Business to business companies know the importance of selling. This isn't a bad thing. It ensures that there is sufficient business to feed the mill – the metaphorical mill – because we know that nowadays many business to business companies provide services, are merchants and don't manufacture things.

This obsession with sales should, in theory, mean that B2B companies are experts at delivering brilliant customer experience (CX). If this is the case, why is the average Net Promoter Score® for business to business companies hovering between 25 and 30 (B2B International, 2017)? (We will be talking about the Net Promoter Score® a lot in this book so if you're not sure what it is, take a quick peek at Chapter 3.)

Successful selling and successful customer experience are very different. A sales-orientated company is geared up to offload as much product as possible into its markets. For sure it will want to keep its customers happy so that they return for more. However, the key thing is to get them to buy products in the greatest volumes, at the best margins. This is most certainly a laudable objective for the sales company. It isn't a particularly laudable objective for customers. The hapless customer may find that once they have signed the order it becomes more difficult to get hold of the salesperson. They may find that once the order has been delivered and paid for it is more difficult to get technical advice. They may find that the company they are dealing with has grown so big it thinks it is doing them a favour selling them a product.

Business to business companies have a long way to go if they want to achieve a Net Promoter Score® of 50 or more. Why is this? We believe that the main reason is because most business to business companies don't have the right culture; they are product led. At some time past their founder entered the market with what was believed to be a great product and it has been pushed in one form or another ever since. Ralph Waldo Emerson did us a disservice with his famous quote 'If a man can write a better book, preach a better sermon, or make a better mousetrap than his neighbor, though he build his house in the woods, the world will make a beaten path to his door' (Natural Histories, 2012). How wrong he is. There are great books, wonderful sermons and brilliant mousetraps lying hidden deep in many woods. Without the right marketing and good customer experience, they will stay there.

You would think that it should be easy to turn a company into a paragon of customer experience. Much of what we will talk about is simple stuff. Here is a starter for ten:

- **Be easy to do business with**: people want to do business with you and they are not looking for a Spartan mud run.

- **Communicate regularly**: don't be shy with your customers. They have chosen you above others and if you have something interesting to say, they want to hear it. Show a personal interest.

- **Be absolutely honest and trustworthy**: integrity in business is everything. Your customers want to know that the promises will be delivered.

- **Show respect**: your customers have a choice. They have honoured you with their business. Let them know you appreciate it.

- **Sort things out**: when problems or differences occur, work them out and do so quickly. Don't leave them to fester.

- **Share dreams**: become a partner. Understand your customers' goals and be proactive in helping achieve them. Do things together.

Does it sound easy? The principles are easy but the execution isn't. Delivering excellent customer experience is a company-wide challenge. All departments in the company need to focus on that goal. Some will feel so remote from customers they will have forgotten that they are there. Also, it would be great if the boss leads the charge and fully commits to customer experience. They have to make it a priority that doesn't get ditched when another business imperative raises its head. If only!

We are father and son. We have run a business to business market research company for nearly 20 years. Between us we have carried out dozens, probably hundreds of customer satisfaction and loyalty surveys. Nearly all these surveys have been for large corporate companies and nearly all have shown that in some way the customer experience in the company is wanting. These surveys have reminded us that great customer experience is built on touching customers' emotions. Setting the right level of expectations, exceeding them, showing kindnesses and engaging with human spirits all create memorable and positive experiences. They exist in business to business markets but they are not as common as they should be.

In preparation for this book we received contributions from many companies and we drew on our experience with many others. Our contributors, without exception, told us that they are on a journey. None believed they were near the end of their journey. They excused their deficiencies by explaining they have only just begun and in every case they emphasized that it is not over. Perhaps it never will be. These champions of customer experience and heroes within their companies aren't looking for perfection but they are never satisfied with what they have achieved. They know that the experiences they provide their customers could be better. We thank them for sharing their stories. They are hard at work constantly seeking to improve the satisfaction of their customers. Their work is hugely rewarding and it will never end. We dedicate this book to them.

As a final note we would like to say that writing this book has been cathartic. It has reminded us of a very important point – business to business relationships are with people not companies. The principles of engagement with our customers should be no different to those we have with our colleagues, friends and families. If we keep that at the front of our minds in everything we do, our customers will stay loyal, work will be enjoyable and our businesses will prosper.

References

B2B International (2017) What is the Net Promoter Score? [Online] available from: https://www.b2binternational.com/research/services/customer-loyalty-research/net-promoter-score-nps/ [last accessed 21 November 2017]

Natural Histories (2012) Historical notes on ecology and evolution [Online] available from: https://historiesofecology.blogspot.co.uk/2012/11/build-better-mouse-trap-and-world.html [last accessed 26 October 2017]

ACKNOWLEDGEMENTS

This book is dedicated to companies that strive to provide their customers with the very best experience. We don't mean an experience that is good nor one that is very good. We mean a customer experience that is so good that customers wouldn't dream of moving to another supplier.

This is an illusionary goal but it is one worth having. We accept that it is not possible to satisfy every customer. It is not possible to make every customer loyal forever. But it is possible to try. In preparation for this book we have had the privilege of having insightful discussions with a variety of businesses that are passionate about improving the experience they give their customers. This book is for all these companies:

Aggregate Industries	Equinix	npower
Air Products	ExxonMobil	Nynas
AkzoNobel	Fenner	Petro-Canada
Ansell	Flogas	Pitney Bowes
Antalis	Fuji Xerox	PPG
Apetito	Gazprom	QBE
AvantiGas	Geberit	RSM International
Baxi Potterton	Grohe	Sage
Berlitz	Grundfos	Samsung
Beumer	Harsco	Seafish
Bibby Financial Services	Henkel	Shell
BP Castrol	IEEE	Speedy Hire
Brammer	International Paint	Stanley Black + Decker
Brenntag	International Paper	Travis Perkins
Brightstar	ITW	Turtle Wax
British Sugar	Jewsons	Vaillant
Brother	Kaspersky Lab	Vandemoortele
Cintas-Berendsen	Kingspan	Vodafone
City & Guilds	Knauf	Wacker
Columbus McKinnon	Kuehne + Nagel	WD-40
Communisis	Leidos	Wolseley
Coveris	Marshalls	Xylem
Dow Chemical	Mastercard	Yodel
Dow Corning	Molson Coors	Zurich Insurance
E.ON	National Instruments	

PART ONE
Why bother?

Customer experience in business to business markets

Like it or not, you are going to have to become more like McDonald's

We want to talk to you about customer experience in business to business markets. If you are reading this book it almost certainly means you are a business to business (B2B) company. We also know that you will be hungry for examples of B2B companies that have succeeded in delivering excellent customer experience. Here we have something of a problem. The larger the B2B company, the worse its performance in delivering excellent customer experience. Furthermore, if you are big and poor at customer experience, you won't want us to tell your story in this book. B2B companies that have failed to deliver excellent customer experience in the past are now under pressure to improve. The pressure comes from our business to consumer (B2C) cousins. There are many excellent examples of great customer experience with the large B2C companies.

The world of consumers and businesses are getting closer. If we can order and receive something from Amazon within 24 hours we start to question why it takes three days for a business to business supplier to answer an email and a month to deliver the goods. When we can get incredible customer service from McDonald's, we wonder why it is so difficult for our business suppliers to do likewise. We will constantly make references to business to business companies in the book and we make no apology for also using examples from consumer markets. This is because we know that consumer companies set the benchmarks and standards by which business to business companies will be judged. You are going to have to become more like Amazon, Zappos, Nordstrom, Chick-fil-A or John Lewis whether you like it or not.

What is customer experience?

We don't leave our emotions at home when we come to work. Customer experience is all about emotions. We know customer experience is just as important to business customers as it is to the general public. It just doesn't seem to get the attention that it should.

Recently, Hague senior (Paul) visited Bradford University to attend a meeting. It was a pro bono get-together and he was happy to join and contribute, especially as Bradford in Yorkshire is his old home town. It was where he was brought up and where he went to school. The meeting was an all-day affair. It finished at 4 pm and he returned to his car to find a parking ticket on the window. It said he had parked illegally and would have to pay a fine of £60, reduced to £30 if he paid within 14 days. Now Hague senior can afford £30. He can afford £60. However, he was incensed at what he thought to be the injustice of the ticket. He ran back to the University building, found the security desk and sought an explanation. He was told he should have had a permit to park though he was unaware of this and the signs on the outside of the car park that gave these instructions were not easily read by someone negotiating their way into it. It materialized that the management of the car parking at the University is subcontracted to a private company and disputes had to be taken up with them in writing (by letter).

Bradford University is a good university, as they all are. The day had gone well and the University had left a great impression – until the discovery of the parking ticket! Paul seethed as he drove back to Manchester. The first thing he did (after he complained bitterly to his wife) was boot up his computer and write letters to various people who worked on security, a Professor who chaired the meeting and the company responsible for car parking. If someone had asked how likely he was to recommend Bradford University on a scale from 0 to 10 where 10 is very likely, he would have given a score of zero.

The purpose of the story is not to denigrate Bradford University. These things happen and the managers of the University would be shocked at the negative effect of the car parking fine. They may think that Paul's reaction was completely unreasonable – which it was. But that is not the point. We all have emotions and they can affect us in funny ways. Sometimes quite minor things, like a feeling of injustice, can get in the way of the big picture. Some small thing that happens at the back end of a meeting or transaction can leave a bad taste with little chance of recovery. In a restaurant we remember the awful coffee far longer than we remember the fabulous starter.

Business to business companies are good at processes. They know how to manufacture things. They know how to shave a penny here and a cent there to make things run more efficiently. They are good at quality control, Six Sigma and logistics. But when it comes to emotions and customer experience, many businesses just leave it to the sales staff. That is not how it should be. Customer experience isn't fluffy stuff. It isn't something for the birds. We will argue that it delivers hard returns; great returns, often much better than any investment in a new milling machine or warehouse. It is just that you can touch a new milling machine and you can walk into a warehouse. Your investment is more obvious. Investing in customer experience is investing in a philosophy. The word 'culture' is going to crop up frequently in our discussions because that is what drives good customer experience. Culture in any company is driven from the top and, being realistic, it isn't always there just as we would want it. However, pockets of culture disposed to delivering customer experience can occur anywhere and, once people see that they are delivering great results, others will want to copy them. A lead from the top is desirable but if it doesn't exist, we will accept a lead from anywhere. It is really important that, through you, we can influence the business leaders. Once they see what it can do to the bottom line, they will be devotees forever.

Learning from the high street

We will frequently discuss what is happening in consumer markets because these are examples we can all relate to. Furthermore, the expectations we have as Joe Public and as Joe Business are getting closer. The conditioning we receive as customers of companies operating in the high street is sure to make us wonder why we can't get the same service or provide the same service in the businesses where we work.

The high street has changed enormously over the last few years. A recent report by the US Department of Commerce tells us that total e-commerce sales in 2016 accounted for 12 per cent of all retail sales (Marketing Land, 2017). In the UK, online sales in 2016 accounted for 17 per cent (Centre for Retail Research, 2017). The online penetration is slightly lower over the rest of Europe though rapid inroads are being made. The web has changed attitudes to customer experience. People no longer have to trail to a shop to make their purchase; they can do so by the click of a button on their phone. The web provides instant experiences, more transparent pricing, easy product comparisons, critical customer reviews and armchair ordering. It became clear in the research we carried out for this book that many of the business to business companies were strongly influenced by B2C companies. The following response was not untypical:

> *'I think there's a brilliant case study out there with Netflix. They get things done. You've got to get the priorities right but then you've got to make things happen. You've got to make things happen locally and then roll them out. Making things happen in our business is the big challenge. We are not yet joined up for this to happen across the whole company.'*

So, there is acknowledgement that we can learn a lot from B2C companies about customer experience delivery. Business to business companies are getting there. They know the importance of customer engagement. Traditionally they have had sales forces making personal visits to customers, developing close relationships, and trying to ensure that customers are fully satisfied. Even if a salesperson isn't calling round to see a customer, there is usually a personal interaction of one kind or another. Someone at a customer service desk will speak to the customer on the phone, someone will email the customer or talk to them about a technical issue. B2B companies have always been customer centric.

Or have they? While it may be true that there is a lot of personal interaction between customers and the business to business supplier, it is usually with one aim in mind – to sell the customer products. This is no surprise. Businesses exist to sell products or services. However, with an emphasis on selling, a company has a very different mindset from one that wants to satisfy the customer's long-term needs. It is why most B2B companies are set up to win business by offering the best package of products, when they are needed, at the right price. These are very functional attributes and it is absolutely essential that every company gets them right if they want to compete in a market. In today's world they are simply not enough. Most companies have good products in the right place at the right price. If this wasn't the case, they wouldn't get a seat at the table. Something different is required to stand out and have the edge over the competition. That something is often emotional and it is triggered by experiences that suppliers can provide.

The problem with business to business companies is that it isn't always consistent. One contributor to the research for the book emphasized this point:

> 'The single biggest challenge we have is consistency and reliability. Getting the perfect experience in B2B isn't a one-off. You have to be able to show, day in and day out, that you value the customer experience. In the B2B environment one bad experience can completely destroy the customer experience even if the previous 99 were very good. One of the things you've got to get right is how you get consistency and how you communicate it across the whole organization. The big question is "how do you get things right time after time?"'

The customer experience we take for granted on the high street and online have become benchmarks by which we judge all suppliers. As consumers of everyday products, it is so easy for us to take our business elsewhere if we are not fully satisfied. This is a huge incentive for B2C companies to try hard to deliver the very best customer service. In general they do and if they don't, the cruel world of economics will see that they improve or go out of business.

Emotions and customer experience

If the products and services we buy meet our expectations, our experiences for the most part stay in the neutral zone. Our expectations are set by the history of our experiences or the promises that a company makes. If we are used to three-week deliveries, we probably wouldn't think to challenge the supplier to ask why we can't receive the product in a week. If we post an out of office notification when we are not at our desk, we are not surprised to receive one from one of our suppliers' sales reps. It is normal.

Business to business suppliers are often privileged in having a greater lock on their customers than consumer companies. B2B suppliers may have contracts with customers that run for a year or so. Even if there aren't contracts in place, a supplier's products may have been tested and approved. Changing to a new supplier can be painful and a problem for the buying company. There is an incentive to stay with 'the devil you know'. Maybe the business to business supplier thinks that the competition will be no different and no better. Business to business companies don't have the motivation to improve a service quality that is 'good enough'. And, to be charitable, they simply may not have learned the skills of delivering service excellence.

Emotions are an indication of what gives us pleasure or pain (Nummenmaa *et al*, 2014). They come to the fore when something happens. Our nervous system becomes aroused and our mental state changes. These changes are automatic. Without thinking, our facial expression will change. If we speak, the tone of our voice is likely to be different. If things get really serious, we could start sweating.

Although there are a huge number of emotions that we suffer or enjoy, a small number summarize most of our feelings:

- Happy and satisfied.
- Excited (which could be both positive or negative).
- Nervous, scared or tense.
- Angry (ranging from irritation through to rage).
- Sad and disappointed.
- Loving, touched or sympathetic.

We shall return many times to the subject of emotions. For now, we just need to know that they are the outcome of experiences. Naturally, our aim is to provide a customer experience that evokes the most positive emotions.

The triggers of emotions

Already you will have noted that in order for emotions to arise, there has to be a catalyst that sets them off. This is at the heart of providing excellent customer experience. We have to have things that generate positive emotions. What might these be?

We have said that a steady state leaves us with no feelings. Emotions need some sort of action or event to trigger them. These events don't have to be earth-shaking. A quick response to an order will make us feel reassured and manage our expectations.

Just the other day we ordered cold pressed rapeseed oil online. Confirmation of the order was immediate, accompanied by a message:

Thank you for your purchase! We do our postal orders once or twice a week, get them all together and box them up and stick the labels on, then one of us takes them down to the local post office and so we don't have to apply a large postal charge we send them out second class. They always get to you but for both of the reasons above I'm afraid it's not an overnight service. It may take a few days so please be patient with us, it will be worth it!

Our expectations were now set up and we sympathized with the reason for the slight delay in the order. The next day another email announced that the order had been shipped and in fact it arrived later that same day. Expectations had been set, were beaten and we were delighted.

When we opened the box, the bottles of oil were safely contained in bubble wrap and a thank you card gave some interesting and reassuring facts on our purchase. We were told that the products were made under careful supervision on the farm. It went on to say the ingredients were natural and, because rapeseed is low in saturated fats, it is good for the heart. All simple stuff and yet validating our decision to buy from a company that was previously unknown to us. The emails and the note in the box had cost the supplier very little. When did you last see a note such as this in anything bought from a B2B company?

Small spoonfuls of delight

Little things can mean a lot. Good customer experience is delivered by managing expectations and adding unexpected delights. The delights need not be much. Good customer experience and strong customer loyalty is built up in small spoonfuls.

Nothing that we have said is ground-breaking and you will all be able to recount similar experiences. But how many of these experiences take place in business to business markets? How many of the orders that you ship include a note giving some interesting fact about your products that will reassure your customer that they are dealing with a great supplier? Our aim is to get you to recognize that great customer experience is dynamic. It must change because it is the unexpected delights that create positive reactions. This means constantly keeping eyes and ears open for new ideas that will mark you out as a company that supplies excellent customer experience.

We are realists. We know that it is a tall order, probably impossible, to provide a constant stream of new delightful experiences week in and week out. There simply aren't enough ideas and in any case, it isn't necessary. We should also be aware that some of the small spoonfuls of delight will irritate a customer if the basics are not being met. Before we can even think of building excellent customer experience, we have to have the right product, at the right price, delivered to the customer in the right way.

We recall a disastrous focus group in which customers had been invited to consider a number of things a supplier could do to add value to its products and services. The moderator running the focus group tried to get the customers to discuss various value-added options. However, the discussion took a bad turn because the supplier that sponsored the focus group was failing to deliver its products on time in full and this was creating big problems. Customers had turned up to the focus group hoping that they would hear how this basic requirement was going to be rectified. The supplier was well aware of the delivery problems and was working on solutions but these weren't easy and were taking time and money. In the meantime, the supplier was trying to achieve some quick wins by introducing small improvements that could add value and would cost little. Unfortunately, customers saw these little things as distractions from what they really valued and couldn't bring themselves to consider them until the basics were sorted out.

Delivering excellent customer experience doesn't require constant hype or marketing initiatives. Nor is it complicated. But it is hard work. It is about focus. Focus on the customer, making sure that we are delivering everything that they need and adding a bit extra. The bit extra, as we will discuss, will not need a huge investment in plant and machinery. However, it may mean a change in mindset in your company. The new mindset will not be confined to the sales and marketing teams. **It must permeate the whole company.** Ideally it should start at the top as this will demonstrate commitment from the company leaders. However, most company leaders have majored in finance or business administration. Not many have risen through the sales or marketing ranks. All company leaders will agree that excellent customer experience is important but they may not have the fanatical devotion to ensure it is prioritized when some other business imperative raises its head. This means that the customer experience initiative, like an amoeba, may have to start in the middle of the company and grow outwards, making converts and proving itself to the rest of the company until all the credit controllers, production people, HR and accounts teams have been brought on board.

The structure of the book

The book is divided into five parts.

Part One: Why bother?

In this first part we explore the benefits of good customer experience. There are a number of links between customer experience, customer satisfaction and customer loyalty. They play in different ways and we should know how they interact. Business leaders will ask why it is necessary to have a fanatical obsession with customer experience and they have every right to ask for proof that it delivers customers with a greater lifetime value and profitability.

Part Two: Mapping the customer experience position today

In order to deliver a great customer experience, we need to know where we stand today. In Part Two of the book we discuss the six pillars of customer experience, which provide the strategy for the programme. The six pillars are commitment, fulfilment (ie, doing what we say we will do), seamlessness, responsiveness, proactivity and evolution.

We also examine the drivers of customer experience and show how great customer experience comes out of good relationships, quick responses and building a company that is easy to do business with. Once we understand the drivers, we need to measure them and particularly to benchmark them so we can see the effect on our business. The benchmarks will be important in helping us see the effect of our customer experience programme month by month or year by year. It will also show how we are performing relative to other companies.

Then we should discuss the customer journey. This is fundamental to customer experience. People's needs vary considerably depending on whether they are at the beginning of a relationship with a supplier or have been customers for years.

Part Three: Strategies for achieving excellent customer experience

Having mapped where we are with our customer experience and developed appropriate measures to use as controls, we now need to set goals for the programme. These goals need to be achievable and set within a timeframe.

With our objectives in place we show how to develop strategies that will ensure that we achieve them. The strategies need buy-in and commitment from leaders in a company and the sales and marketing teams that will deliver the experience. We discuss the importance of bringing the internal teams on board and creating a culture of customer orientation that is necessary if the strategy is to work.

Customers are not all the same. These differences lead us to the importance of recognizing different groups of customers and having strategies appropriate for each segment.

Part Four: Implementation of a customer experience programme

Implementation is often the most difficult task in business. We discuss how branding, product positioning, price, channel to market and promotion play a vital role in the customer experience programme.

In business to business marketing, relationships are of crucial importance. We consider the role played by people in addition to the 4Ps and branding.

Part Five: Controls that ensure the customer experience programme stays on track

Delivering an excellent customer experience is a never-ending race. For that reason, we need to constantly monitor, change and improve our processes. In Part Five we show how to track performance over time and how to keep reinventing the process so it is forever fresh.

Things to think about

At the end of each chapter there are a number of questions to think about. At this early stage ask yourself the following questions:

- What is the appetite for a customer experience programme in your company? Where is the main drive and initiative of this programme coming from?

- What is prompting the interest in customer experience in your company? To what extent is it prompted by a desire to win more loyal customers, beat the competition or improve profitability?

- How strong are the emotional links between your customers and your company? How have these emotional links developed? How consistent are you in developing them?

References

Centre for Retail Research (2017) Online Retailing: Britain, Europe US and Canada 2017 [Online] available from: www.retailresearch.org/onlineretailing.php [last accessed 3 October 2017]

Marketing Land (2017) Report: E-commerce accounted for 11.7% of total retail sales in 2016, up 15.6% over 2015, February [Online] available from: http://marketingland.com/report-e-commerce-accounted-11-7-total-retail-sales-2016-15-6-2015-207088 [last accessed 3 October 2017]

Nummenmaa, L, Glereana, E, Harib R and Hietanen, JK (2014) Bodily maps of emotions, *Proceedings of the National Academy of Sciences*, **111** (2), pp 646–51

Exploring customer experience, loyalty and inertia

Satisfaction and loyalty

Above all else we want our customers to be loyal. Loyal customers are our best salespeople. Loyalty creates devotion and devoted customers love to talk about suppliers and why they are so great. With loyal customers you hardly need salespeople. A customer who sings your praises and recommends you as a supplier has far more credibility than someone who you employ. A customer who is loyal returns time and again, and over a lifetime spends a significant amount of money with you. We can become obsessed with large customers. This is understandable; a big customer makes a big difference to revenue. Dealing with two or three large customers may be hard work but it's easier than dealing with 100 small ones. However, if we lose a large customer, we are left with a big hole.

In 2005 PortalPlayer enjoyed significant business with Apple who bought its specialized semiconductors for the original iPod. At the time its chief executive said it was 'well positioned for the year ahead' thanks to its strong relationship with its leading customers. Just four months later, Apple switched to another supplier. PortalPlayer's stock lost half its value overnight (Bradshaw, 2017) and in 2007 it was acquired for $357 million by Nvidia Corporation (Nvidia, 2017). Up until 2005 PortalPlayer would have considered Apple to be one of its most loyal customers. In fact, such was the dependency that PortalPlayer had on Apple, it accounted for 90 per cent of its revenue. Loyalty, desirable as it is, can't be relied on. It has to be earned and it has to be nurtured. You may think that your relationship with your customer is rock solid while all the time the customer could be talking to another supplier that is making a promise and offering a price that is throwing loyalty to the wind.

Let's move to the other extreme and consider Archer's Bakers in Marple, the small town where we live. They have hundreds of customers, none of them large or dominant. Archer's bread and meat pies are famous and on Christmas Eve a queue extends far outside the shop as people wait patiently to receive their orders. Each week the average customer spends only a few pounds in the shop. However, loyal customers do this every week and many of them have been doing so for years. It would not be difficult to find a good number of customers who have spent well over £1,000 at the shop so far in their lifetime and they keep returning to buy more. Loyalty brings with it a value which, spread over a large number of customers, can be much more secure than PortalPlayer's business with Apple.

There are many Archer's in business to business markets, small companies providing software services, manufacturing castings or offering advertising services. They are run by proprietors and families that know their customers, and will move heaven and earth if asked to do so. To these small companies the subject of delivering excellent customer experience is obvious and fundamental. They depend on a loyal customer base and they will do everything to make sure it stays that way.

This raises the subject of what drives loyalty. For sure, a customer must be satisfied. It is hard to think that a dissatisfied customer will stay loyal for long. However, satisfaction alone isn't a guarantee of loyalty. Amazon does a great job and receives high satisfaction scores from its customers. This does not mean to say that its customers are entirely loyal to the company. It is 'The Everything Store' but no one buys everything from Amazon. When it suits, we spread our business around and buy from other suppliers even though we are satisfied with Amazon. A loyal customer would not be so promiscuous with their buying habits.

The starting point of loyalty requires the customer to receive an offer that is as near perfect as possible in terms of the price, the product and the place where it is sold. These are the basics that we expect and we want them to be delivered to our expectations every time we make a purchase. If one supplier proves consistently good at these basics while competitors are unreliable, this could in itself make customers loyal to the consistent company. However, it would be unusual because in most markets there are many alternative suppliers and most offer a similar standard. This being the case there needs to be something extra to create loyalty and that something extra is very often a people thing.

Where there is a strong personal relationship with the supplier, there is a good chance there will be a high level of loyalty. The relationship that

Apple had with PortalPlayer was strong for a number of years and during that time it could be said there was a high level of loyalty. The problem for PortalPlayer was simply that it was too dependent on Apple because loyalty, as strong as it may be, does not last for ever.

When milk was delivered to the door, people stayed loyal. They knew their milkman or milklady personally. Those up early would see them making their rounds. Others would see them as they knocked on the door to collect their money every week. They valued the reliable service, which from time to time would be in difficult weather conditions in the middle of winter. People did not regularly switch their milk delivery person. The relationship was strong but it did not guarantee loyalty. Conditions change. Supermarkets offered large bottles of milk with a shelf life of over a week at prices that the milk delivery people could not beat. Mums and dads, going to work, were not at home to bring the milk inside on a hot day. This decline in the use of doorstep milk deliveries doesn't detract from the fact that for many years people were extremely loyal to their milklady because they valued the personal service.

Loyalty to businesses

People like doing business with people and this is a good basis for building loyalty. But, is it possible to be loyal to a company? This is a crucial question as our interest is in how we can use customer experience to build B2B loyalty. Wikipedia begins its treatise on loyalty as follows (Wikipedia, 2017):

'Loyalty is devotion and faithfulness to a cause, country, group, or person. Philosophers disagree on what can be an object of loyalty as some argue that loyalty is strictly interpersonal and only another human being can be the object of loyalty.'

In this definition there is no mention of loyalty to a company. However, companies are made up of people and just as there is loyalty to a milklady, there is a loyalty to individuals within an organization. Furthermore, companies develop brands and these stand for something. Over time brands become a sort of cause and this engenders loyalty. We talk more about the role of brands and customer experience in Chapter 14.

In reality B2B customers appear far more loyal than the general public. It is not unusual for a business to business company to have customers that have been buying from it for more than 10 years. This is loyalty of a kind but not in the true sense of the word. It is not a faithfulness and devotion that cannot be broken. Most business to business companies are fearful of placing all their eggs in one basket. They very often buy from two or three suppliers. This means that a B2B supplier may believe it has the devotion of a customer when in fact it is a split loyalty with the business being divided between a number of different suppliers. We have seen how Apple's devotion to PortalPlayer was blown away when someone thought there was a better alternative.

Take banks for instance. It is not unusual for a bank to have customers who have dealt with it for years. Some of the bank's customers may be dissatisfied, or at least not particularly satisfied, though not to the point where they are prepared to go through the pain of moving to a different bank. Effectively, they are hostages to the bank. Someone who remains a customer in such circumstances is taking the line of least resistance despite failings in the bank's service. Not only does change require effort, the customer may feel that a different bank wouldn't necessarily be any better.

This spurious loyalty is common in business to business markets. Many customers continue to do business with their suppliers through inertia; it is easier to carry on as always rather than go to the trouble of seeking a new supplier. A switch to a new supplier may require approvals, new service level agreements, and have the necessary financial arrangements in place. After all that, there is still the worry that the promises of the new supplier may not be met.

Recovering lost loyalty

What is a loyal customer? We have seen that Apple appeared to be a loyal customer of PortalPlayer and indeed it was – until things changed. At the end of the day Apple's loyalty is mainly to itself. If it believes that it can obtain better products or a better business deal, the loyalty is blown away.

If we find that a customer has used the same supplier for 10 years, does that mean it is loyal? During the 10 years, the customer may have dealt with two or three additional suppliers, checking each against the other to make sure that the best price and delivery is achieved. The business that is shared between the different suppliers could be changed all the time. What seemed like loyalty may have been a tactical play on the part of the customer.

Let us examine the factors that break this apparent loyalty and what can be done about them:

Messing up: every supplier makes mistakes from time to time. Products can fail, deliveries may be late, people may fail to do what they said they would do. It is important to recognize that these things will happen and that there is a procedure for sorting things out. The first and obvious thing to do is to rectify the problem. This will require effort and incur costs. The rectification must be quick and efficient. A customer who faces a problem is unlikely to tolerate a delay in having it sorted.

Second, it is almost always important to apologize profusely. Some people find this hard, especially if they believe that the failure wasn't entirely their fault. The legal eagles in the supplying company may worry that an admission of failure suggests that they were at fault and open the company to litigation. 'Sorry' sometimes seems to be the hardest word. However, there isn't a more straightforward way to apologize and it almost always will appease the customer. We are not talking about saying sorry in the way airlines do when there is a delay. We know they don't care when they say 'sorry for the inconvenience' because they say it all the time and the inconveniences keep happening. There has to be a genuine sense of contrition in the apology.

This brings us to the third thing to do when something is messed up; fix it and do something special. It is what is called '+1' in customer experience. It is adding something. Whatever is added matters. If the hotel where you stayed on business messes up and offers you a free night stay for one person on a weekend, it is worthless if the location would never be visited again. If, however, you are offered a free night at any hotel in the entire chain, it would have more recovery value. When a company corrects a problem and does it with panache, it can leave a customer thinking more highly of the company than it did before. This is referred to as the Service Recovery Paradox (McCollough and Bharadwaj, 1992). It is a paradox that a customer experience disaster, followed by a profound apology, a swift rectification of the problem and a +1 addition will be so much appreciated, customers think even more of the supplier than they did before.

Competitor offers a better deal: there is always a supplier that will offer to do something cheaper and better. It is quite surprising that with temptations such as these, customers don't move more frequently. They undoubtedly have learned that the promises made by would-be suppliers may come to naught and the risk of change isn't worth it.

That said, customers can and do play the market and some will move around. Three marketing professors, Kumar, Bhagwat, and Zhang, studied this subject and suggest that it is possible to target specific lost customers who have a high propensity to return (Kumar *et al*, 2015). They found that customers who defect because of price can be won back and stay longer than they did in the first instance. If the customer left because of poor service, they are more difficult to retrieve. They also found that offering the lost customer a new bundled package, such as a better price together with a tailored offer, was more successful than simply offering a healthy price discount.

Customer experience and moments of truth

In 1981, Jan Carlzon was made CEO of Scandinavian Airlines (SAS). The company was making significant financial losses and had a reputation for always being late. Carlzon's priority in his new role was to get the basics right. Within a year, SAS had moved from being 14th out of 17 airlines in Europe for its punctuality to being number one. He changed the centralized command and control nature of the company to one that put decision making in the hands of customer-facing staff. This proved not only to be a great boost for staff morale, it also meant vast improvements in customer service. In early 1984 Air Transport World named SAS 'airline of the year' for 1983. The company turned itself round by improving customer experience. The story was told by Carlzon in his book, *Moments of Truth* (Carlzon, 1987). These moments of truth were every occasion when a customer came into contact with an SAS employee. In a service company such as an airline, they can add up to many millions of occasions a year. They are called moments of truth because they determine whether the company will succeed or fail in the eyes of the customer. As Carlzon said, '*They are the moments when we must prove to our customers that SAS is their best alternative.*'

Airlines provide fertile ground for stories on customer experience. An airline that has built its brand and reputation on providing a great customer experience is Southwest Airlines. The story of this company is described in the book *Nuts!* (Freiberg and Freiberg, 1998). A colleague of ours told of the following experience on a Southwest flight.

'We were in mid-flight with Southwest when a passenger left his seat to visit the bathroom at the back of the plane. The air stewardess stood up in the aisle and told everyone that it was the passenger's birthday. She asked everyone to shout "Happy Birthday Jim" as he walked out of the bathroom. The air stewardess then made Jim a birthday hat out of drinking straws, which he proudly wore for the rest of the flight. On the same flight, the pilot had introduced himself in person before leaving the gate, telling everyone face-to-face what the journey time would be and that it would be a smooth flight. It was nice to see the face of the person flying the plane! This is what I would call a truly personal company.'

Herb Kelleher, the founder and CEO of Southwest has stamped his personality on the airline. It is not unusual for Southwest staff to sing the safety announcements. Kelleher's starting point is to get the right people into the company. He tasks his People Department with finding hires with a sense of humour. He said '*I want flying to be a helluva lot of fun!*' He is of the view that you hire attitude and train skills.

Don't think it is easier for an airline to create a great customer experience than a business to business supplier. There are plenty of airlines that perform badly in their delivery of customer experience. It is usually the large national and legacy airlines that seem to find it beyond their powers to give discretion and authority to their customer-facing staff. Customers are subjected to sour faces, bullying instructions and are given the impression by the airline staff that the whole process of operating the airline would be much better if only there weren't any paying passengers. Why do we see considerable parallels here with large B2B companies?

Ryanair has even achieved significant publicity and notoriety out of its poor customer service. In 2014, Siegel+Gale surveyed over 12,000 customers in eight countries and found Ryanair to be the second worst ranked brand on ease of customer use of a company's products, services interactions and communications (Magrath, 2014). The boss of the airline, Michael O'Leary, hit back with the question '*Then why are we the biggest airline?*' He had a point. It is possible to be large and successful if the product delivers all the basics, even if the customer experience is poor. Ryanair's popularity has been won with its bargain basement prices and good timekeeping.

The ignominy of being named and shamed at delivering such poor customer experience must have rankled. Perhaps it also made Ryanair ask itself whether, with a bit more tender loving care extended to customers, it could be even more successful. This appears to be the case because, at the time of writing in 2017, Ryanair announced initiatives for year three of its 'Always Getting Better' programme, which aims '*to improve all aspects of the customer experience*' (Ryanair, 2017). The published financial results in 2016 suggest that improved customer experience is paying off, so much so that David Bonderman, Ryanair's Chairman, made the following statement in the company's 2016 financial report that announced an 80 per cent increase in profit after tax – '*The past year has seen our profitability grow strongly while we enhanced our product and service further in year 2 of AGB (Always Getting Better)*' (Ryanair, 2016).

Things to think about

- Do you know the loyalty of your customers?
- To what degree is this loyalty rock solid in your favour rather than shifting from time to time to other suppliers?
- Do you have a process for recovering lost customers? How effective is this?
- How many of your customers split their business between you and your competitors? What is your share?
- What would it take for you to have 100 per cent of your customers' wallet?
- What is it that you do that satisfies your customers? What is it that you do that makes them loyal?
- What are the moments of truth for your customers? How are you performing on these moments of truth?

References

Bradshaw, T (2017) The blessing and curse of being an Apple supplier, *Financial Times*, 7 April [Online] available at https://www.ft.com/content/3d49b76a-1b76-11e7-a266-12672483791a [last accessed 12 February 2018]

Carlzon, J (1987) *Moments of Truth*, Harper Perennial, New York

Freiberg, K and Freiberg, J (1998) *Nuts! Southwest Airlines' crazy recipe for business and personal success*, Broadway Books, New York

Kumar V, Bhagwat Y and Zhang A (2015) Regaining 'lost' customers: The predictive power of first-lifetime behavior, the reason for defection, and the nature of the win-back offer, *Journal of Marketing*, 79 (4), pp 34–55

Magrath, A (2014) Ryanair named second-worst brand in the WORLD for customer service (but AXA insurance comes top of the poll) [Online] available from: www.dailymail.co.uk/travel/travel_news/article-2812512/Ryanair-named-second-worst-brand-WORLD-customer-service-AXA-insurance-comes-poll.html [last accessed 3 October 2017]

McCollough, MA and Bharadwaj, SG (1992) The recovery paradox: An examination of customer satisfaction in relation to disconfirmation, service quality, and attribution based theories, in *Marketing Theory and Applications*, ed Chris T Allen, American Marketing Association, Chicago

Nvidia (2017) NVIDIA® Acquires PortalPlayer® [Online] available from: www.nvidia.com/object/portalplayer_acquisition.html [last accessed 3 October 2017]

Ryanair (2016) Ryanair Annual Report, FY16 [Online] available from: https://investor.ryanair.com/wp-content/uploads/2016/07/Ryanair-Annual-Report-FY16.pdf [last accessed 3 October 2017]

Ryanair (2017) Always Getting Better [Online] available from: www.ryanair.com/gb/en/useful-info/about-ryanair/always-getting-better [last accessed 3 October 2017]

Wikipedia (2017) Loyalty [Online] available from: https://en.wikipedia.org/wiki/Loyalty [last accessed 3 October 2017]

Understanding customer experience and profitability 03

Company attitude, customer experience and memories

Michael O'Leary, CEO of Ryanair, once taunted his customers with threats of charging them if they use the toilets on his planes. These threats were never carried out and maybe they were never intended but they did signal an attitude. It is the attitude that the customer should feel honoured that they are able to use the services and products of the supplier rather than the supplier feeling privileged to have the patronage of the customer.

They are also memorable experiences or comments and memory drives experiences. If we remember a bad experience at a hotel we are unlikely to return. It is the same with businesses. An unpleasant call or a confrontation with an unyielding sales agent will undoubtedly cause a reaction. If this experience occurs at the beginning of the customer journey, when someone is considering doing business with the company, it could result in a premature severing of relationships. At the time of writing, one of our colleagues was seeking a legal firm to act on a merger and acquisition. They phoned a number of lawyers who had a strong reputation in M&A and asked if someone would return the call as soon as possible. Out of five lawyers that were phoned, only one returned the call and they were appointed.

Colin Shaw of Beyond Philosophy (Shaw, 2017), says that the only way to build customer loyalty is through customers' memories. Emotions drive memories. The problem is that we often don't know what emotions customers are feeling during their journey with a supplier; we don't know when they hit a peak or a low point and we don't know how they feel when the customer interaction is over. We can ask people about their emotions but they are sometimes hard to describe. They also can fluctuate greatly from one occasion to another. Difficult though this may be, it is something that we need to understand and measure so be prepared for us to return to the subject in Chapter 7.

One of the biggest problems we face in delivering excellent customer experience is that most customers don't tell us how they feel. We've all sat in a restaurant, chatting away to our friends or colleagues, when a waiter passes by and asks 'is everything alright?' Nine times out of 10 people say 'yes, everything is fine'. In fact, it may not be. The food may not be quite right, the people at the next table may be too noisy, the service may not have been fast enough. That said, things were not so bad and it would look churlish to complain, so we don't. The restaurant owner is left with the impression that customers are happy, but they don't really know how they feel. Do your customers think that you are easy to deal with? Do they like your sales rep? Are there some little things that irritate them that they haven't told you about? Business to business customers can be more taciturn than customers in a restaurant. At least the customers in the restaurant have been asked if they are satisfied.

If you don't know what is wrong, it is very difficult to put it right. There has to be recognition that it is possible to do things better. It is the starting point of the customer experience initiative. One of our contributors to the book was extremely honest:

'Customer experience does not mean a lot to people in our company at the moment. It's purely a transactional topic. We are quite good at what we do today in a transactional sense but we don't add a great deal on top. Customer experience is not a concept that is well-known in our company and because we are B2B, people need to be convinced by the science. I want to draw a distinction between traditional customer service and customer experience and I am not there yet.'

This isn't unusual in business to business companies. In most B2B companies there are pockets of people who believe in customer experience and want it to permeate the whole organization. Some will believe that is a simple question of getting everyone to 'have a nice day' while others know that it is a complete culture change.

The service profit chain

It is said that there are only three ways to increase profits – to sell more, to charge more or to reduce costs. This is broadly true although James Heskett, a professor at Harvard University, believes that there is a fourth way. In his book, *The Service Profit Chain* (Heskett *et al*, 1997), Heskett and his colleagues argue that profits begin with satisfied employees. Satisfied employees work hard to deliver a great service to customers who will be satisfied, stay loyal, buy more from the company and generate more profits. Intuitively this makes sense.

Fortune magazine lists the best places to work (*Fortune*, 2017). At the top of the list, for the eighth time in 11 years is Google – a company that achieves high scores in customer satisfaction and loyalty, and is super profitable. Out of the top 20 companies on the *Fortune* 100 list, six supply software, five supply financial services and four supply professional services. There are only three manufacturing companies, one is in biotech, one in medical devices and the other in construction. If this doesn't add up to 20 it is because there is another one in grocery and one in hospitality. The key point here being that manufacturing companies and merchants are few and far between.

The paucity of business to business companies as examples of the service profit chain means that we have to choose another consumer example to explore the principle. Taco Bell examined its employee turnover records across its many stores and discovered that the 20 per cent of stores with the lowest employee turnover had double the sales and 55 per cent higher profits than the 20 per cent of stores with the greatest employee turnover (Heskett *et al*, 2008). Happy employees stay with a company, which reduces hiring costs as well as generating satisfied and loyal customers.

We should stop there. The Taco Bell story confirms what we want to believe. The problem is that there are lots of studies on this subject and they are sometimes delivering conflicting results. For example, a study described in the *International Journal of Hospitality Management* in 2009 (Chi and Gursoy, 2009) indicated that while *customer satisfaction* has a positive significant impact on financial performance, *employee satisfaction* has no direct significant impact on financial performance. Is this because the world of hospitality management employs different people to Taco Bell? Is it because you can still get reasonable levels of satisfaction with indifferent staff and good processes? We should take note of the wise words of Chris Daffy, one of the customer experience gurus who contributed to our thinking:

'There needs to be someone in an organization, preferably a leader or at least someone with influence, who really has conviction. They need to really believe that if we focus properly on looking after our customers, all of the other bits and pieces will fall into place. You see this in the Dorchester Group. Chris Cowdray is Chief Executive Worldwide of the Dorchester Hotel Group, and he says "Listen folks, if we look after our guests in a way that they just don't get at any other hotel in the world, they'll keep coming back." And they do.

What you don't want is someone who says "Can we do a cost justification on this?" My soul goes "Goodness me. This person just doesn't get it." I remember Tom Peters once screaming from a conference stage "If you have to cost justify delivering exceptional service to your customers, you shouldn't be in that job."'

Be that as it may, leaders do need to justify business initiatives and there will always be requests for determining the relationship between Net Promoter Score® or customer experience and financial results.

The link between customer satisfaction and loyalty can be used to assess revenue at risk. Customers who award supplier satisfaction scores of 9 or 10 out of 10 and give a score of 9 or 10 out of 10 to the question 'how likely are you to recommend this supplier?' are likely to be rock solid in their loyalty (or as much as can be expected given the experience of PortalPlayer described in Chapter 2). Customers giving lower scores on a scale from 0 to 10 are in varying degrees of risk of defection. A survey of customers who are asked how satisfied they are and how likely they are to recommend a supplier can be mapped to show revenue at risk (see Figure 3.1).

Customer satisfaction and return on investment

Good waiters know the link between profitability and good customer experience. They know that if they deliver excellent service they are more likely to be generously rewarded than if they serve the meal with an imperious or disinterested attitude.

What is so obvious at a micro level is more difficult to recognize at a company level. CEOs, eager to show strong financial returns every quarter

Figure 3.1   Example of revenue at risk based on levels of satisfaction and likelihood to recommend

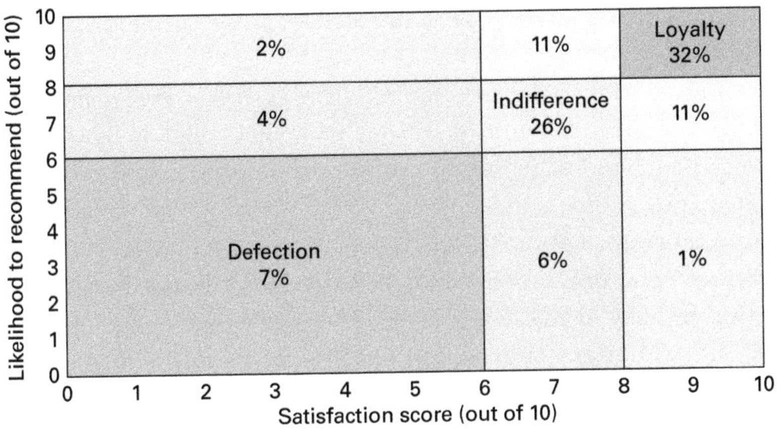

SOURCE Created based on theory by Heskett *et al*, 1997

may not be so interested in the indulgent customer experience argument that promises a long-term payback. One way to convince the higher echelons of management is to demonstrate the relationship between customer satisfaction and financial performance over time. The link can be obscured by the lag between an improvement in customer satisfaction and increased revenues and profits. Early work on this subject was carried out by three academics, Eugene Anderson, Claes Fornell and Donald Lehmann, who used a database of 77 large Swedish firms participating in what was known as the Swedish Customer Satisfaction Barometer (SCSB) (Anderson *et al*, 1994). Financial data was available on each company.

The academics found that if customer satisfaction increased 1 per cent per year over five years, there would be an increase in profitability of 11.5 per cent over that period. While they were confident they'd found a robust link between improvements in customer satisfaction and profitability, they had some caveats.

They did not find an automatic link between an improvement in customer satisfaction and an increase in market share. When companies supply a specialized niche it is easier to achieve higher satisfaction scores than companies that supply a broad spectrum of customers and have a large market share. Those companies with a large market share will inevitably have a spread of customers who receive a diluted offer and therefore do not receive the accolades that are more readily given to the specialists.

However, the authors conceded that '*in undifferentiated industries with homogeneous customer preferences, it is more likely that customer satisfaction and market share are positively related, especially in the long run*' (Anderson *et al*, 1994). That sounds like many business to business companies!

In summary it is easier to offer excellent customer experience if you specialize. Larger and more dominant companies find it hard to win customer plaudits, but if they do so over a long period, they will win market share.

They also pointed out that expectations have a big impact on customer satisfaction. At the time of their work, the Mercury Tracer and the Mazda 323 were two virtually identical cars made different by their badges. However, the Mazda customers were more satisfied because they had different expectations from the car. We can see how expectations influence satisfaction in many other areas. An expensive wine served in cut glass goblets will be perceived better than if it is served in a blind test in plastic cups. Brands carry perceptions and they too influence satisfaction. We will discuss this subject at greater length in the book (see Chapter 14).

Net Promoter Score® (NPS) and growth

The Net Promoter Score® is a simple metric that is derived from the following question:

> *How likely are you to recommend supplier X on a scale from 0 to 10 where zero means not at all likely to recommend and 10 means very likely to recommend?*

The Net Promoter Score® (NPS) is calculated by subtracting the proportion of people that give a score of 6 or below from the proportion of people that give a score of 9 or 10 out of 10. This score is the invention of Fred Reichheld, a consultant at Bain & Company. Bain & Company claim there is a strong correlation between Net Promoter Scores® and growth. They say that in most industries, Net Promoter Scores® explain between 20 and 60 per cent of the variation in organic growth rates among companies. Their figures suggest that, on average, an industry's Net Promoter leader will outgrow its competitors by over 200 per cent. The NPS is a particularly strong indicator of growth in mature markets where there are a number of players (NPS, 2017).

Having a high NPS is just the start of achieving a financial payback. Companies must make it easy for customers to buy more. They must encourage their customers to tell colleagues and friends of the things that make the company so great. Customers of business to business suppliers don't necessarily interact with each other very often. It may be helpful to find ways to increase the interaction by creating user groups and offering stories so they can more readily tell colleagues about the excellent experiences served up by a supplier. It is the reason why exhibitions and seminars are favoured by business to business companies. They are fertile grounds for spreading customer recommendations.

Customer satisfaction and diminishing returns

If you are hungry you will very much appreciate a good meal. There may be a point in the meal where you have had enough. You will have eaten plenty and to eat more would not improve your view of the meal. Could it be the same with customer satisfaction?

In 1998, two academics at Wharton School, University of Pennsylvania, Christopher Ittner and David Larcker, published research on a survey of 2,500 business customers of a telecoms company (Ittner and Larcker, 1998). They found that once the average customer satisfaction score exceeded 7 out of 10, customer retention levelled off. They also found that the link between growth in revenue from customers began to level off once the company hit an average customer satisfaction score of 8 out of 10.

This makes sense and it is worrying. It indicates that beyond a certain point, there are diminishing returns from improving the customer experience. The danger is that, recognizing this levelling off of customer satisfaction scores after achieving an average of 8 out of 10, leaders of a company will see no point in further investment in the initiative.

We know that good customer experience requires financial investment. IT systems and processes need to be in place to connect departments and record customer activity. These are necessary to make the customer journey seamless, quick and efficient. There will be a requirement to invest in training to ensure that staff understand the importance of delivering customer satisfaction and how to achieve it. It may be necessary to be forgiving and lenient with customers who complain, even if you know they are in the wrong.

The point is that once the processes and systems are installed, once the training has been carried out, nearly everything else is down to attitude. From that point on there will not be a need for a huge investment. Delivering amazing customer experience is achieved by the flick of a switch in the mindset of staff. Fostering and encouraging this attitude is vital. It would be dangerous if a company loses this momentum just because it has reached the point where their customers are saying 'we really do like you as a supplier'. It would be like turning off the engines on an aircraft that is cruising at 35,000 feet. Just because it has got to this level doesn't mean it will stay there without further power. We should remember that just offering good customer experience is forgettable. Only exceptional customer experience is remembered, discussed and shared (see Figure 3.2).

When a company is making great strides in the 'need to improve' zone (see Figure 3.2) everyone is enthused. The customer satisfaction index moves quickly north and is rewarded by a positive change in customer purchases.

The 'hard to improve' zone moves beyond getting the basics right. This is where the company needs to join its processes and break down the silos within the business. Success will continue to bring an increase in customer purchases year-on-year.

Then we reach the zone where customer satisfaction scores are averaging more than 8 out of 10. The company has proved itself to be a customer experience champion. Customers are delighted and say 'wow'. This is one of

Figure 3.2 The wow/complacency gap

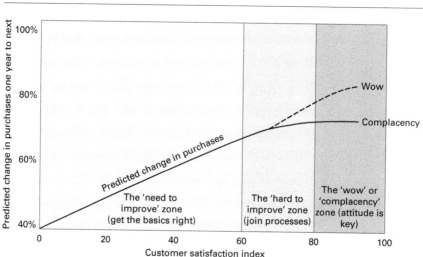

the most dangerous zones of all because it can lead to complacency. A car needs a foot on the pedal to get it to a high cruising speed and the foot needs to stay on the pedal if the speed is to be maintained. So it is with customer experience.

Things to think about

- Do you really know how your customers feel about your products and service? How can you be sure?
- What do you do for your customers that leaves them with positive memories?
- How happy are your employees in the work that they do? How satisfied are your customers? What links can you see between the two?
- What proportion of your customers are truly loyal – ie, rating you 9 or 10 out of 10 on satisfaction and 9 or 10 out of 10 on likelihood to recommend?
- Will your company only pursue a customer experience programme if it knows the financial return?
- Are you caught in the complacency zone where you feel that more effort is required to raise or even maintain customer satisfaction?

References

Anderson, EW, Fornell, C and Lehmann, DR (1994) Customer satisfaction, market share, and profitability: Findings from Sweden, *Journal of Marketing*, 58 (3), pp 53–66

Chi, CG and Gursoy, D (2009) Employee satisfaction, customer satisfaction, and financial performance: An empirical examination, *International Journal of Hospitality Management*, 28 (2), pp 245–53

Fortune (2017) 100 Best Companies to Work For 2017 [Online] available from: http://fortune.com/best-companies/ [last accessed 21 November 2017]

Heskett, JL, Jones, TO, Loveman, GW, Sasser, ES and Schlesinger, LA (2008) Putting the service-profit chain to work, *Harvard Business Review* [Online] available from: https://hbr.org/2008/07/putting-the-service-profit-chain-to-work [last accessed 3 October 2017]

Heskett, JL, Sasser, E and Schlesinger, LA (1997) *The Service Profit Chain: How leading companies link profit and growth to loyalty, satisfaction, and value*, The Free Press, New York

Ittner, CD and Larcker, DF (1998) Are nonfinancial measures leading indicators of financial performance? An analysis of customer satisfaction, *Journal of Accounting Research*, **36** (supplement), pp 1–35

NPS (2017) How the Net Promoter Score® Relates to Growth [Online] available from: http://www.netpromotersystem.com/about/how-is-nps-related-to-growth.aspx [last accessed 3 October 2017]

Shaw, C (2017) New Research Reveals Lack of Customer Understanding [Online] available from: https://beyondphilosophy.com/new-research-reveals-lack-customer-understanding/ [last accessed 3 October 2017]

PART TWO
Mapping the customer experience position today

The six pillars of customer experience

The customer experience recipe

In their book *Raving Fans!*, Ken Blanchard and Spencer Johnson tell us that the starting point of developing great customer service is to visualize what it will be like. They call this the 'decide what you want' moment. This is your chance to create a dream that will turn into reality. They emphasize that not all customers will buy into your vision. That is okay because we know it isn't possible to please everybody. It is important to please your target customers. Following this visualization of your offer and matching it with the desires of customers, they say that you now have to deliver your promise +1. They are taking us back to the subject of meeting and beating expectations (Blanchard and Johnson, 2011). Delivering the promise is meeting the expectations and the +1 is adding something else that turns an ordinary experience into an extraordinary one.

Visualizing customer experience isn't easy. What should be the building blocks of this utopian customer experience? Julia Cupman is a director of B2B International, a company that specializes in business to business market research. From the many studies she has carried out, she has concluded that six ingredients should be included in any customer experience programme (Cupman, 2016). We will discuss the detail of how they are delivered in later chapters but for now let's take a look at these crucial pillars. They are:

- **Commitment:** delivering excellent customer experience takes time. It requires patience, investment and the belief that it is worthwhile. Whoever is in charge of the customer experience programme has to have absolute faith that it is the way forward. When times get tough, money is short and it is easy to slip into compromise mode. There must be a commitment to deliver excellent customer experience – come what may.

- **Fulfilment:** words are cheap and theories are interesting. However, actions are required if excellent customer experience is to be achieved. Customers have expectations when they do business with a company and they want to see that what was promised is delivered. Customers want every customer experience to be fulfilled consistently, not just once or twice, but every time. It is usually the hardest part of any programme.

- **Seamlessness:** doing business with a company should be pleasurable. A company that is difficult to work with will not deliver excellent customer experience. Difficult companies are those that believe the complications of serving the customer should be shared with the customer. Customers are passed between departments, becoming frustrated and exhausted. Customers do not want to know about the internal difficulties faced by the company; they want a purchase process that is seamless and easy.

- **Responsiveness:** doing business with a company inevitably involves inter-actions and communications. Communication can be face-to-face, by telephone, email, text or letter. The communications could be information about a product, acknowledgement of an order, assurances of deliver-ies, etc. They must be quick and timely. Customers have become used to quick responses in other aspects of their daily life and this requirement has become an essential ingredient in excellent B2B customer experience.

- **Proactivity:** excellent customer experience is achieved by going beyond expectations. This requires a high level of imagination and proactivity in order to make the experience better, different, faster or cheaper.

- **Evolution:** 'If you always do what you've always done, you will always get what you've always got.'[1] Staying the same means going backwards as inevitably competitors catch on to good ideas and copy them. Customers get used to service, and what is considered excellent customer experi-ence today will seem 'old hat' tomorrow. The customer experience recipe needs to be constantly changing and improving.

As with any recipe, it is possible to vary the ingredients and still deliver something that tastes great. There is usually a sequence in the recipe for introducing each ingredient. We have listed them in the order that we believe is important. Commitment is the starting point and there needs to be lots of it. Very quickly the customer experience needs to be made tangible with the qualities of fulfilment, seamlessness, responsiveness and proactivity. Because customer experience is an ongoing process, evolution will need to ensure that it is freshened up.

Figure 4.1 The performance of large B2B companies on the pillars of customer excellence

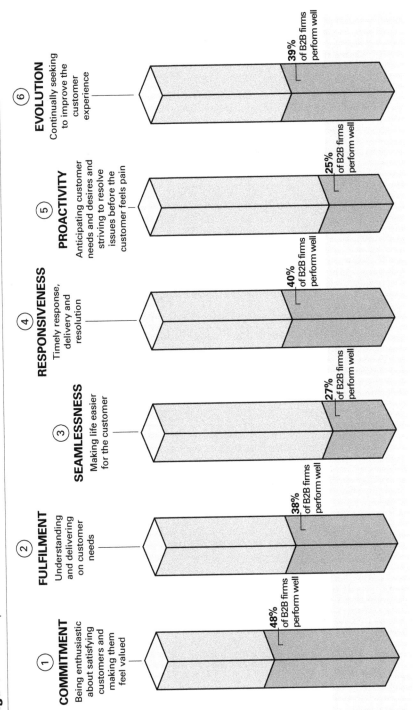

① **COMMITMENT**
Being enthusiastic about satisfying customers and making them feel valued

48% of B2B firms perform well

② **FULFILMENT**
Understanding and delivering on customer needs

38% of B2B firms perform well

③ **SEAMLESSNESS**
Making life easier for the customer

27% of B2B firms perform well

④ **RESPONSIVENESS**
Timely response, delivery and resolution

40% of B2B firms perform well

⑤ **PROACTIVITY**
Anticipating customer needs and desires and striving to resolve issues before the customer feels pain

25% of B2B firms perform well

⑥ **EVOLUTION**
Continually seeking to improve the customer experience

39% of B2B firms perform well

SOURCE Used with permission from B2B International

In 2016 B2B International carried out a survey of 200 large corporate organizations and found that less than half the respondents believed their companies were performing well on each of the ingredients required to deliver excellent customer experience (see Figure 4.1).

Commitment

For a company to be able to deliver excellent customer experience time after time, it needs commitment and, if possible, this should come from the top. According to Jeffrey Sanders, writing in *Forbes*, around 30 per cent of *Fortune* 500 CEOs begin their careers in finance. Only 20 per cent of CEOs in these large companies start out in sales and marketing roles (Sanders, 2011). Could this focus on finance and lack of experience in sales and marketing be a reason that commitment is often lacking?

CEOs have the difficult task of deciding how they will maximize a return on investment and there are never limitless funds. A CEO with a financial background may be harder to convince of the return on investment from a customer experience programme than a CEO who has risen from the ranks of sales or marketing. As we discussed in Chapter 3, the link between customer experience and return on investment (ROI) is sometimes difficult to establish as there may be a time lag between the instigation of the programme and the money flowing in. This could partly explain why only a half of large B2B companies believe that their organizations are fully committed to delivering customer experience. A contributor to this book acknowledged the importance of this support from the top.

'The starting point for us was around 2014. The board of our company recognized there was something really big around Net Promoter Score® and opportunities for growth. When we started in 2014 our aim was to get a baseline on what the customer was experiencing at that time. Also, we had people who were getting involved in lots of other aspects of customer experience such as customer segmentation.

We then moved on to think about how we could get some real measures that could help us achieve change. We moved from insight into getting measurements that enabled us to turn the dial on these priorities. This was a step change for us.

We had a change of leadership and this resulted in an acceleration of our customer experience programme with NPS and customer satisfaction becoming our number one priorities. It also resulted in investment in some of the things we needed to do to improve the customer experience – for example increasing our stock of products against customer needs.'

Commitment has to be more than words. In April 2017, United Airlines hit the press following the heavy-handed eviction of a passenger from an over-booked flight waiting to depart from Chicago's O'Hare airport. Amateur videos of the event showed the passenger being dragged down the aisle of the plane as he was forcibly ejected. It was all the more difficult for Oscar Munoz, United's CEO, to explain how this happened when the strapline of the company is 'Fly the friendly skies'.

Of course, almost every company would acknowledge that they should deal courteously with their customers. They would accept that they have a responsibility to make the experience of dealing with customers as pleasurable as possible. However, this is not as easy as it would appear. Creating great customer experience has a cost and, more importantly, it requires an attitude of mind. Funds are often in short supply but getting the right attitude of mind can be even more difficult.

Furthermore, it is easy for large companies, especially the people at the top of an organization, to become distanced from their customers. A visit by a large company CEO to a customer can become an act of theatre. Customers are carefully chosen, maybe even briefed on what to say. Large companies can be very powerful and some have got used to wielding that power. They may believe that they know what is best for customers and use their size to impose their views. It isn't long before large companies start to impose terms and conditions on their suppliers and say they will not pay bills for 60 or even 90 days – take it or leave it. They have credit control conditions for customers with a script from lawyers rather than the customer relations department. This can easily create a culture of dominance that spills over into the way they behave with customers. We have all been in situations where, as customers of a large company, we have felt that the organization resents our presence.

In contrast, small companies and new start-ups are desperate for business. They will do almost anything to please their customers. The proprietor will stay up overnight getting an order ready. They will risk their necks travelling through deep snow to make sure it is delivered. Their emails are signed off with various telephone numbers and details encouraging contact (something seldom apparent in an email from an employee of a large company). Small companies know the importance of being totally committed to customers. This doesn't mean that they are perfect in delivering excellent customer experience. Small companies are sometimes capable of cutting corners to save money or to get the job finished. If this is at the expense of quality and safety it will be a disaster as these basics should never be compromised in an eager attempt to deliver a great customer experience.

In an ideal world, support for the customer experience programme should begin at the top. If there is no high-level support, all is not lost. It is possible to start delivering excellent customer experience at grass roots level. In a survey we carried out for one of the largest chemical companies in the world, a customer told us why they continued to buy from the company:

> 'If it wasn't for Tony, I wouldn't buy from XXX. I call Tony and he makes things happen in his company. He works magic. He does it quickly and without fuss. I don't know how he does it, I am just glad that he is there for us.'

Tony is a salesperson for the chemical company and in the eyes of the customer he is a hero. As a result of his work with customers, keeping them satisfied, he is a top salesperson and earns lots of money. Other people in the sales team see what Tony does and what makes him successful. They emulate him and it isn't long before other members of the sales team have created their own excellent customer experience programme. It is a virtuous upward spiral.

The opposite is also possible. If the sales team is disillusioned they will have negative feelings and it won't be long before the gloom spreads to customers. Managing the culture of commitment is a vital part of any customer experience programme. As the management guru Peter Drucker is reported as saying, 'culture eats strategy for breakfast'.

Fulfilment

Fulfilment is making sure that what is promised is delivered. People have an expectation when they buy something and they must feel that the expectation is fully met. And what is fulfilled must be consistent. It must be delivered to the same standard not once, not twice, but every time. This vitally important ingredient is often the responsibility of low-ranking people within an organization. It is the role of waiters in restaurants, checkout staff in grocery stores, receptionists and customer service desks that take orders. The television programme, *Undercover Boss*, takes high-level corporate executives from the comfort of their offices and puts them in customer-facing jobs within their companies to find out how things really work. The experience is usually revealing for the executive who finds out how difficult it can be to please customers and how hard it is to do so for eight hours a day. The demanding job is not well paid, training is often minimal and the customer-facing employees may have limited authority.

The fulfilment of customer experience requires people who can empathize with the customer and, if necessary, can own and solve customers' problems. These people need to be fully committed to delivering customer experience. It is hard to see how this can be the case if empathy isn't a condition that is required when they are recruited or if customer delight isn't part of their job specification or if they aren't empowered to use their own discretion.

Fulfilling great customer experience is made difficult by the varied needs of customers. Some customers are easy-going while others are difficult and demanding. Some want a simple no-frills transaction while others want and expect bells and whistles. While standing at the checkout in the grocery store the cashier may engage in a pleasant discourse with the customer being served, to the frustration of the people in the queue who are mumbling 'get on with it' under their breath. Keeping one person happy may make five people in the queue unhappy. Knowing how to deal with the wide cross-section of people in a business to business situation requires considerable interpersonal skills. Just consider the way a sales rep has to deal with the needs of different customers.

John is a sales rep for oils and greases used in industrial lubrication. A typical customer call starts with doughnuts for those on the shop floor at 8 am and a check that all is well with the machines that use his lubes. He then calls on the procurement manager to make sure that all is well with the service level agreement. If necessary he will return in the evening to entertain the leadership team in a restaurant of their choice, where he will be expected to share the latest news on what is going on in the industry.

Seamlessness

A customer checking in at the airport may not understand that the people who put their bags on the plane and the people responsible for the plane leaving on time do not work for the airline. As far as the customer is concerned it is all part of the flying experience.

In the same way, when someone phones a business to place an order they do not think about the processes that are involved. Computer systems must be in place that check if the product is in stock. The production line has to be scheduled to make the products. The customer needs to have their details logged into the system and approved before a transaction can take place. There are numerous processes within every organization that determine whether the customer receives a seamless experience. Customers become frustrated when a sales clerk begs forgiveness for the slow service because 'our computers are down'. A customer does not want to hear that someone in the technical department isn't available right now. They do not want to hear that their order will have to be put in a queue because others, presumably more important, are ahead of it.

Doing business with any company requires effort and this comes at a price. The quicker and easier it is to do the business, the better the customer experience. Companies such as Amazon have set a standard that demonstrates how easy it can be to place an order. They create reference points that customers use when measuring their experience with other suppliers. The silo mentality is a barrier to great customer experience in many companies, as one of our respondents explained:

'What are the difficulties in delivering excellent customer experience? If people say "where's that stuff I ordered?" it may take us a week to investigate and we might have to say we don't know what went wrong or why it went wrong. How do you engage people to be customer focused? We have team briefings, newsletters and a lot of information on our intranet. People are working in teams to get the job done. But they work in stove pipes and we need to knit these together. I think the teams are genuinely customer focused but sometimes they are thinking just of their team. Sometimes it is a question of getting people into a conference room and getting them talking about customers and their needs so that somehow it all joins up.'

Responsiveness

Speed is of the essence when delivering excellent customer experience. People expect to be quickly put through to a sales order clerk or an enquiry desk. They do not want to listen to automated instructions, which may be convoluted, unclear and in the end send them to the wrong department. They do not want to hear that staff are busy, that they are the fifth in line or that the estimated delay will be 20 minutes. In the general scheme of things 20 minutes may be neither here nor there but when someone is anxious and juggling lots of other balls, it is 19 minutes too long.

Speed of responsiveness is expected. We want an acknowledgement of our order as soon as it is placed and we want delivery in days, not weeks or months.

Zappos, the online shoe company, has a deserved reputation for excellent customer experience. The company has built a huge amount of trust with its '365 days to return' policy. BJ Keeton, a keep-fit fanatic and web designer from Alabama, tells the story of the purchase of a pair of Asics Nimbus 14 running shoes from Zappos, which turned out to be too narrow. Even though the original packaging had been binned (Zappos require the original packaging as part of their returns policy), the Zappos customer service person was happy to accept the returned shoes, agreed to immediately send out a bigger size, issued a $35 refund because the price of the shoe had dropped, and upgraded the customer's account to lifetime VIP status so that they could always have free next-day shipping.

Stories such as this build trust in a company's responsiveness. Some people will take advantage of a generous returns or complaints policy but this is likely to be far offset by the goodwill it generates.

Proactivity

Customers expect their suppliers to be proactive. They are eager for proactivity. When asked how a business to business company can improve its products or services it is not unusual for customers to say they want more frequent contact.[2] This, despite complaints of too many unsolicited emails and cold calls. Contact of the right kind is welcome. This could be calls to check that all is well, to share latest trends in the market or to talk about updates on new products.

Customers expect their suppliers to be one step ahead in understanding their needs. Of course, they want the products they buy to be better, faster and cheaper but they, the customers, don't know how this can be achieved. Their faith is in the supplier working towards these ends, in which case they will be rewarded with a greater market share.

Proactivity demands a deep understanding of a customer's business. In order to suggest something new or a co-development programme, a supplier must know how this will impact the customer. It means getting close to the customer. In a recent workshop with a client that makes food ingredients, the marketing director made the following rant:

'I walked into one of our storerooms the other day and a table was groaning under the weight of pens, Post-it notes and giveaway collateral that we send out to customers. I am sure there isn't one single customer who is waiting eagerly to receive one of our branded pens. Their desks are littered with them. We spend €50,000 a year on this crap. That would buy us a food safari on which we could take 10 of our largest clients to one of our factories and spend the next two days on a gastronomic tour where we could jointly discover and talk about food tastes. Now that would be a great experience and a great opportunity to get close to important clients.'

Evolution

What was once considered a delight and a novelty soon becomes expected. Flying business class for the first time is exciting. Those who do so regularly soon become critical of points of detail. The airlines attempt to keep ahead of customers' needs with roasted nuts, special foods and comfortable flat beds. However, there is a limit to the alcohol that can be served, the number of times hot towels can be proffered and the amount of goodies that can be pushed into an amenity kit. Friendly, smiling and attentive service will almost always be the most valued ingredient in the excellent customer experience package.

Smiling and personal attention will never go out of fashion. It is important to offer little surprises as well. Thinking back to Chapter 1, it is the spoonfuls of delight that can be memorable. Some years ago, the wife of one of the authors of this book took delivery of a new BMW car. The car was much admired by her friends and she was frequently asked what she liked about it. She never thought to mention the M43 engine with a displacement of 1895 cc, which produces up to 118 hp. She never mentioned its economic fuel consumption or its sporty heritage. All she could say was 'it has a rechargeable torch in the glove compartment – don't you think that is fantastic?!'

It is the little things that often make a difference.

Keeping the subject of customer experience fresh in the company that is pushing a customer experience initiative is also a challenge. It isn't long before people get tired of seeing another set of NPS and customer satisfaction scores. It is same old, same old, especially if there is very little change from one wave of results to another. There needs to be an evolution in the way that the results are communicated. After a time, the numeric scores become numbing but the stories of customer experience never tire:

> 'If I've only got five minutes with one of our leaders I want to know what five slides I should share with them. I just share five slides. We have an NPS of 65 to 70 so we don't talk about that a great deal any more. We talk about the "why". We talk about what else is in the data.'

The power of storytelling was mentioned by a number of contributors to the book:

> 'One of the biggest challenges of our business is to tell our proposition story really, really well. It is difficult to get consistent communication of our proposition across the whole of our business. Anecdotes get shared across the company and they become folklore. These stories on the street become really powerful in the company, even more important than the survey results that we have. For example, we introduced free coffee in one of our depots recently and it was very well received by customers. Within minutes of this initiative being introduced into the branch it was shared throughout the whole company. If you have good stories they spread like wildfire and they get adopted. The reverse is also true. If it's a bad news story it gets spread very quickly and is difficult to contain.'

Free coffee for the company is a quick win and it appears to work wonders for building customer satisfaction. It can be quickly rolled out through all the other depots and then the company must face the challenge of 'what comes next?'

Things to think about

- Do you have a vision of what you would like your customer experience to be?
- Do the six pillars of customer experience fit your company? Which do you consider to be most important?
- How would you rate your company's performance on each of the six pillars?
- Which is a priority for improvement?

Notes

1 Attributed variously to Anthony Robbins, Albert Einstein, Henry Ford and Mark Twain.

2 In a survey of food ingredient buyers, those who received a call (visit or phone call) from their account manager every week gave a customer satisfaction score 13 per cent higher than those who received a call once a quarter.

References

Blanchard, K and Johnson, S (2011) *Raving Fans! A revolutionary approach to customer service*, HarperCollins, London

Cupman, J (2016) The Six Pillars of B2B Customer Experience Excellence, *MarketingProfs*, 26 April [Online] available from: http://www.marketingprofs. com/articles/2016/29806/the-six-pillars-of-b2b-customer-experience-excellence [last accessed 16 February 2018]

Sanders, JS (2011) The path to becoming a Fortune 500 CEO, *Forbes*, 5 December 2011

Essential metrics 05
for measuring
customer
experience

Our discussion of customer experience so far has described how impressions are created by events that take place between the supplier and customer. Constant improvements to customer experience require measurements. Peter Drucker, the management guru, is cited as saying 'What gets measured gets managed' (Prusak, 2010). We need to think about what to measure and how to do so. We will begin with a consideration of what is available to us as metrics, some internal and others external.

Internal measures of CX

Most of the measures that we will discuss in this chapter are based on customer ratings. Before we turn to these external scores, it is worth noting measures that are easily and inexpensively available because they exist within a company.

Employee satisfaction (the score achieved on this metric should be high): happy employees are more likely to deliver excellent customer experience than those who are dissatisfied. Measures of employee engagement are, therefore, a good predictor of customer experience. Employee satisfaction surveys are commonplace nowadays and vital for understanding the culture of a company. It is important that employees are able to feed back honest views on what it feels like to work at the company and so any survey should be anonymous and confidential. Employee satisfaction surveys are relatively easy to carry out using inexpensive tools such as Survey Monkey, SurveyGizmo, QuestionPro and Key Survey.

Employee absenteeism (this metric should be low): not all employee engagement measures require a survey. For example, it is easy to measure employee absenteeism. Who is regularly off work? When are they off work? And most importantly, why are they off work?

Voluntary work (should be high): another indication of strong employee engagement may be the amount of charity work carried out by people within the company. Employees with a mindset of helping others are likely to have a mindset of helping customers.

Product returns (should be low): the amount of product returns is an indication of product quality and undoubtedly will influence customer experience. This is a metric that hopefully is at a minimal level.

On time in full (OTIF) (should be high): delivering products on time and in full is another measure of a well-run company and this should be as near as possible to 100 per cent.

Increased sales (should be high): it may seem simplistic to suggest that sales revenue is a measure of customer experience. To some degree the trajectory of sales revenue is a reasonable clue as to customers' experience. Of course, sales revenue is also affected by the performance of the product, its price and promotion. If sales are falling there could be something wrong with the product, the price, the promotion or the customer experience.

Complaints (should be low): every company should have a complaints procedure. A company doing everything in its power to be perfect could still receive complaints. Feedback from customers on what they dislike about a company is valuable material. The problem is that 9 out of 10 customers leave for a competitor when they have poor experience without ever issuing a complaint (Drehmann, 2013).

The number of complaints will itself be an indicator of customer experience. An uptick in the number of complaints would suggest something is amiss. The ease with which complaints can be made is an indication of a company's attitude to providing excellent customer experience. It demonstrates a willingness to listen and react positively to criticism.

Most complaint forms allow customers to describe their grievance and this usually involves verbose descriptions of events. It is worthwhile analysing these verbatim comments and grouping them into themes that show failures of product quality, price problems, delivery problems, customer service and the like.

Customer churn (should be low): companies lose customers for various reasons. Some customers change their processes and no longer need the product they have bought for years. A customer may suffer a decline in sales of its products and so require fewer component products from its suppliers. There could be a change in technology that results in a substitute taking the place of the product. However, most lost customers are the result of dissatisfaction with a supplier or the belief that another supplier can do better. This creates the churn rate, which is the lost customers expressed as a proportion of the total number of customers in a year.

A survey carried out in 1997 by The American Society of Quality Control, determined that two thirds of customers (by far the largest proportion) changed supplier because of the indifferent attitude of their existing supplier and not because of failures in quality or dissatisfaction with prices (*San Francisco Business Times*, 1997). We have no reason to believe that this figure has been reduced.

In business to business markets churn rates are usually quite low. A company supplying components or raw materials could have a churn rate of less than 10 per cent and usually it is nearer to 5 per cent. In some fickle markets, such as telecoms, it will most probably be higher.

Loyalty programme participation (should be high): loyalty programmes are not the preserve of hotels and airlines. Any company can run a loyalty programme, encouraging customers to see themselves as part of a club, with associated privileges. The number of members of the club and their participation provides an indication of strong customer experience.

Repeat business (should be high): customers who return again and again to buy from a company can be assumed to be receiving good experiences. It is not unusual in business to business markets to find customers who have bought from the same company for five years or more. We should be careful here in believing that repeat business is always an indication of good customer experience. It could be inertia on the part of the customer. A change in personnel who specify and buy the product or some aggressive activity from a competitor could destabilize the regular custom.

Customer and employee referrals (should be high): a strong indicator of good customer experience is advocacy – recommendations from other customers or employees. Whenever a new customer is brought on board it is worth asking how they heard of the company and if it was through a referral of any kind.

Other internal measures: there may be other measures within a business that provide clues about customer experience. The conversion rate of proposals/quotes to orders could offer a clue about customer experience at the front end of the customer journey. Other measures, small though they may be, could be the number of unsolicited letters of praise and commendations that are

Table 5.1   Internal metrics for customer experience

Subject	Metrics/KPIs	Benefits
Employee engagement	Employee satisfaction	Spin-off is strong CX
	Employee absenteeism	Reduced cost of recruitment
	Employee voluntary work outside of formal hours	Develops a culture of mutual help
Quality	Product return rates	Reduced cost of defect and error rates
	Delivery timeliness	Lower cost of returns
Customer satisfaction	Increased sales	Lower costs through increased scale
	Customer complaints	Lower complaint costs
Loyalty and advocacy	Customer attrition/churn rates	Reduced upsell and cross-sell costs
	Loyalty programme participation	Lower retention costs
	Repeat business	Increase in lifetime value
	Customer and employee referrals	Lower cost of sales acquisition

received about staff. Table 5.1 provides a summary of internal metrics that can be used for quick and inexpensive indications of customer experience.

Websites such as www.glassdoor.com provide comments and ratings from employees who have worked at a company. Although this is not a direct measure of customer experience, it provides an indication of the culture of the company.

External measures of CX

Internal measures usually need supplementing by metrics from customer surveys. There are a number of these metrics, each providing different insights into customer experience.

Net Promoter Score® (NPS)

The Net Promoter Score® or NPS was developed by Fred Reichheld of Bain & Company and has become a standard measure of customer experience. The score is based on answers to a simple question:

How likely are you to recommend brand X (or company X) to a colleague using a scale from 0 to 10 where zero means not at all likely and 10 means very likely?

The score is computed by taking the percentage of people who give a score of 9 or 10 out of 10 (called 'promoters') and subtracting the percentage of people who give a score of 6 or below (called 'detractors'). Crucially, those giving a score of 7 or 8 are ignored (passives).

The ratings to this question are seen as a synthesis of customers' experiences. The score will be driven by perceptions of the quality of the product and the value for money as well as softer factors such as brand and customer service. A high Net Promoter Score® is a strong predictor of growth of the company and we shall discuss typical benchmarks in the next chapter.

Care must be taken when using the Net Promoter Score® (NPS). When asked this question, many business to business customers give scores of 7 or 8 out of 10. These scores indicate that a company is performing acceptably though it is not outstanding. They are not included in the calculation of the NPS score. This means that if, say, 50 people are asked the question, 30 may be ignored in the calculation if they give a score of 7 or 8 out of 10, in which case the NPS calculation is based on only 20 responses. If comparisons of NPS scores are made between different companies or if the NPS is a tracking metric, year on year, it can fluctuate wildly depending on the small number of responses provided by promoters and detractors. A total of 50 responses is usually deemed to be the minimum number to obtain a reliable NPS score.

Customer satisfaction score

Customer satisfaction scores are the bedrock of customer experience measurements. They have been tried and tested over years. People understand what it means to answer a question that asks:

How satisfied are you with company X on a scale from 1 to 10 where 1 means not at all satisfied and 10 means very satisfied indeed?

Answers to this question correlate strongly with the mean Net Promoter Score®.

The simple customer satisfaction score question can be asked for a company as a whole and for various aspects of its products and services. For example, surveys typically ask how satisfied people are, using a scale from 1 to 10, on quality, on delivery, on order taking, sales representation, etc, as well as how satisfied they are with the company in general.

The scores on the different aspects of product and service can be correlated with overall satisfaction to determine what is driving customer satisfaction. If the scores given by most customers for one of the attributes is high and most people also give a high score to overall satisfaction there is a prima facie case for an association between the two figures. Similarly, low scores for an attribute and low overall satisfaction scores suggest a link between the two sets of data. We discuss this in more detail in Chapter 7 where we examine what individual attributes drive customer satisfaction.

Customer effort score

A paper in *Harvard Business Review* in 2010 assessed the Net Promoter Score®, the customer satisfaction score, and the customer effort score as predictors of customers' likelihood of repurchasing from a supplier (Dixon *et al*, 2010). The authors found that the customer effort score outperformed the other customer service metrics. The question they posed was:

> *How much effort did you personally have to put forth to handle your request?*

Of the customers who reported low effort in dealing with a company, 94 per cent said they would repurchase from the company.

The question is useful and could be made simpler and easier to ask in different languages (for an international study) if couched as follows:

> *How much effort is required to do business with company X on a scale from 1 to 10 where 1 means a significant amount of effort is required and 10 means very little effort is required?*

The customer effort score is relevant for some products and services more than others. An airline buying a new airliner will expect to spend a good deal of effort on the purchase process. However, many business transactions are at a lower level and suppliers are valued when they are easy to deal with. Amazon make 'ease of doing business' a key part of their value proposition with their 'one click' order facility.

Net value score

We live in a competitive world, so it is not enough to know how we are performing in *absolute* terms; we need to know how we are performing in *relative* terms. This necessitates comparative scores on overall satisfaction and NPS with other companies in a competitive set. Such comparisons

Figure 5.1   Plotting companies on the value equivalence line using the net value score

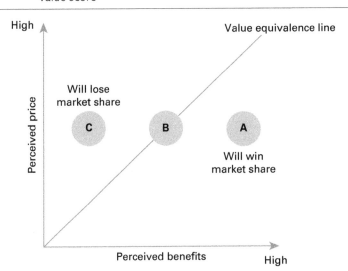

show to what degree a company is better or worse than other companies at satisfying customers. The usefulness of the net value score is that two simple questions allow us to plot a company's position on the value equivalence line (see Figure 5.1):

How would you rate company X on the product or service benefits the company offers, compared to the product/service benefits offered by other suppliers of similar products/services?

How would you rate company X on its prices, compared to the prices of other suppliers of similar products/services?

The net value score shows to what extent customers perceive that a company offers more or less value for money than others in the same marketplace. It is a good indicator of future growth and potential actions. For example, company A in the diagram is offering more benefits than companies B and C for what is perceived to be a similar price. It is therefore in a position to pursue its current pricing strategy and increase its market share, or raise its price and collect more profits.

These customer metrics play to different strengths and all have their place in a customer experience programme (see Table 5.2).

Table 5.2 The role of external CX metrics

Metric	Question	Where to use it
Customer satisfaction score	On a scale from 1 to 10 how satisfied are you with company X?	Determines strengths and weaknesses of a company on different aspects of its customer value proposition
Net Promoter Score®	On a scale from 0 to 10 how likely would you be to recommend company X?	Establishes loyalty to a company and is an indicator of its growth and profitability
Customer effort score	On a scale from 1 to 10 how much effort is required to do business with company X?	Indicator of ease of doing business and future market share
Net value score	How would you rate company X on its products or services compared to other similar suppliers? (And similarly how would you rate it on its prices?)	Positions a company on the value equivalence line

The metrics can be used to compare different companies, compare different strategic business units and to track performance over time. They will indicate to what extent action is needed and to what extent any attempts to improve customer experience are having a positive effect.

Open-ended comment

The quantitative metrics are useful for benchmarking and tracking. They do not provide the underlying reason for the scores. This calls for open-ended questions. Wherever possible, after each of the rating questions, an additional question should be asked: 'Why did you say that?' The verbatim answers to this question will indicate why someone would not recommend a company, why they are not satisfied, why a company is difficult to do business with and so on. Equally, the 'why?' question will explain the reasons for a strong performance.

Answers to the question 'why?' can be superficial. Someone who gives a low score on satisfaction and is asked 'why?' may answer in very general terms – 'I don't like the company, I don't like their service.' Additional probing is needed to find out what aspect of the service isn't liked or if there is something more fundamental about the company that is causing the dissonance.

It is not unusual for a low score on satisfaction to be the result of personality clashes between customer and supplier. For this reason, most customer satisfaction surveys are carried out by independent market research companies who offer confidentiality and anonymity to all respondents.

Goals for customer experience

The customer experience measures show the views of customers at a point in time. These measures can be used to track changes and to set targets for improvement.

It would be hard to see how anyone within an organization would argue against the principle of improving customer experience. Improved customer experience generates more loyalty, increased sales, justifies premium prices and leads to improved profitability. The evidence for this has been set out in Chapter 3.

Let us assume that a company has carried out a survey and arrived at measures that show current customer satisfaction levels are 7.8 out of 10, the Net Promoter Score® is 22, and the customer effort score is 7 out of 10 (where 10 is 'very easy to do business' and 1 is 'not easy at all to do business'). These are baselines that can be tracked in the future. However, it will be necessary to have more specific goals to make sure they move in the right direction. If customer feedback says that a company is failing in speed of response, some specific goals could be set to rectify this perception, such as:

- The number of times that the phone is answered within three rings.
- The speed with which orders are acknowledged by email.
- The percentage of orders that are fulfilled on time and in full.
- The percentage of orders that are fulfilled within a couple of days, a week, 14 days, etc.
- The percentage of complaints resolved within a couple of days, a week, 14 days, etc.

Goals for different groups

We know that customers are different and have different requirements. Some want a quick, no-frills transaction while others expect high levels of engagement and service. In order to achieve excellent customer experience scores it is necessary to understand the way customers segment and to respond to them appropriately. The many dozens of segmentation studies carried out by the authors lead us to suggest that within a group of business to business customers 20 to 30 per cent of customers want a transactional offer with low prices and minimal service. Another 20 to 30 per cent may expect very high levels of service, while the rest want something in between. Each of these sizeable customer segments needs addressing differently and it will be necessary to develop an offer that consistently serves their preferences. Building an organization that can readily move between these segments is discussed further in Chapter 13.

Total quality management and customer experience

Total quality management (TQM) is a philosophy and a business process to ensure that an organization delivers the highest level of quality. Some companies seek to achieve TQM through processes such as ISO 9000 or Six Sigma (the number of defects per million products). Whatever the method used for TQM, its purpose is to continuously satisfy customers' needs. Within a typical TQM culture, everything is geared towards customer satisfaction by getting it right first time. The processes of TQM will ensure as near perfect quality as possible, timeliness in dealing with customers and deliveries, ease of doing business, value for money and so on. It will also have built into it procedures for continuous improvement on the grounds that customers' needs change and competitors will almost certainly be responding to meet those needs. The foundation of TQM is the application of quantitative methods that use measurements to improve all the processes within a company so that they meet or exceed customers' needs.

Things to think about

- What internal measures are you using to measure your customer experience performance?
- What use are you making of complaints? Are they seen as a pain or a gift?
- What external measures are used to measure customer experience?
- Which external measures are most appropriate to meet your customer experience goals?

- Do you understand what is driving your customer satisfaction and customer experience scores? How can you get deeper insights into what customers think beyond the numeric scores?

- Do you set targets for improving customer experience? What is the basis for setting these targets? Do you track your performance on these measures?

- Where does total quality management fit into your customer experience programme? How could it be used to improve customer experience?

References

Dixon, D, Freeman, K and Toman, N (2010) Stop trying to delight your customers, *Harvard Business Review*, July/August, pp 1–7

Drehmann, D (2013) Complaints Are Gifts..., *Customer Experience Magazine* [Online] available from: https://cxm.co.uk/complaints-are-gifts/ [last accessed 3 October 2017]

Prusak, L (2010) What can't be measured, *Harvard Business Review*, 7 October [Online] available from: https://hbr.org/2010/10/what-cant-be-measured [last accessed 3 October 2017]

San Francisco Business Times (1997) The top reason customers leave, *San Francisco Business Times*, 19 October

How to benchmark customer experience

What to benchmark

Our aim when delivering customer experience should always be excellence. Business to business companies don't have a spectacular record in this regard. Most are mediocre in their performance. Being better than the competition does not mean a lot. Indeed, it can lead to apathy generating the belief that if you are better than the competition it is good enough. Our aim should be to set targets that are realistically high, even if much higher than poor-performing competitors.

'No man is an island.' No company stands in isolation. The companies that you *may* be judged against could include companies that customers use in their daily life. When someone buys a product from Amazon and it is delivered to their door the same day, when they obtain cash from a cash machine at any time of day, when they pay their bills at the push of a button, and when they have a Big Mac and a drink in their hands in McDonald's in less than a couple of minutes, they may wonder why it takes a business to business supplier 48 hours to reply to an enquiry.

Benchmarks are important because they provide reference points against which to judge performance. At face value, a customer satisfaction score of 7 out of 10 seems quite good. It is certainly some distance beyond 5, the apparent halfway point of the scale. However, when customers are presented with a scale from 1 to 10, where 1 is a low level of satisfaction and 10 is the highest level of satisfaction, most respondents give scores of between 7 and 10. A company would not stay in business for long (unless it had a monopoly) if it had an average customer satisfaction rating of 6 or below. Think about it. If you were asked to rate your satisfaction with your dentist and you gave them a score of 6 or below, we would expect you to be looking around for a new one.

In fact, an average score of 7 out of 10 on satisfaction is relatively low and yet most business to business companies have customer satisfaction scores of between 7.5 and 8.0. An average score of around 8 out of 10 is good. Average scores of over 8 out of 10 are very good and it becomes increasingly difficult to improve average scores by 0.1 or 0.2 once a score of 8.5 out of 10 is achieved. An average score of 9 out of 10 would mean that over a third of customers are awarding scores of 10 out of 10 which is tantamount to saying that the company is perfect, a status that is rarely achieved in business to business markets.

A company seeking to improve the delivery of its customer experience is no different to someone setting out to run a marathon. The athlete is obsessed by two benchmarks – their personal best and their performance against others in the race. A runner almost always checks their watch when setting out on a training run. However, the motivation to raise performance will be greatest on the day of the marathon. That will be the occasion when they set their sights on beating others who are taking part. There will be dozens if not hundreds of runners in the race and only an elite few will lead the field. Those who finish last are not losers. They have proved themselves capable of running the 26.2 miles and this in itself is a huge achievement.

So it is in business. Delivering excellent customer experience is a marathon. In fact, it is a race that never ends. It requires energy, dedication in training and a real desire to do the very best, whatever that may be. A company that sets out to deliver excellent customer experience is setting itself apart from those who are not participating in the race.

Benchmarking metrics

In Chapter 5 we discussed a number of metrics that can be used to measure customer experience. There are a few to choose from – the Net Promoter Score®, the customer satisfaction score, the customer effort score, and the net value score are among the favourites. The choice of measure is very much determined by its purpose. If a company believes that it needs to improve 'ease of doing business', then the customer effort score would be an important measure. If the board of a company wants a performance score to compare with other companies, it may make sense to use the Net Promoter Score®. It is quite normal to obtain two or three measurements on satisfaction as they each measure different things.

Although there are a few different ways we can measure customer experience, the customer satisfaction score, using a scale from 1 to 10, is a standard in most benchmarking surveys. There are a number of reasons for this:

- It is widely used, with lots of published data for comparison.
- The score works well with small samples.
- Respondents understand the concept of satisfaction whereas 'effort' and 'likelihood to recommend' may not always be appropriate.
- It is easy to ask about overall satisfaction and specifically about satisfaction with particular aspects of the product, price and service.
- Correlating overall satisfaction scores with satisfaction scores on individual aspects of a company's offer will indicate where action is required to improve customer experience.

In the UK and the US there are two organizations that make customer satisfaction scores available across a range of industries:

- ACSI (American Customer Satisfaction Index) http://www.theacsi.org/
- UKCSI (UK Customer Satisfaction Index from the Institute of Customer Service) https://www.instituteofcustomerservice.com/

In each case customer satisfaction scores are shown out of 100 though the questions are asked on scales from 1 to 10 or from 0 to 10. (It is worth noting that because most people use the right-hand part of the scale – from 6 through to 10 – it doesn't matter whether the scale begins at 1 or 0.)

Published satisfaction scores from UKCSI show that British retailers, as a group, achieve scores of 82 out of 100, insurance companies receive scores of 79 out of 100, and utilities and telecoms have scores of 74 out of 100. Within each of these industry groups there is a wide range of performance scores for the companies that are included.

Scores from the American-based ACSI show similar levels. For example, US grocery companies have average satisfaction scores of 78 out of 100, life insurance companies achieve an average of 79 out 100 and telecoms companies score a mean of 71 out of 100.

Although these are examples from consumer markets, they indicate how most customer satisfaction ratings fall within the corridor of 70 to 80 out of 100 (ie, respondents gave scores of between 7.0 and 8.0 out of 10 on the scale used in the interview question).

In both the US and the UK, Amazon achieves one of the highest satisfaction scores of around 87 out of 100 while in the US fast food retailer

Chick-fil-A and the supermarket, Trader Joe's, achieve similar scores (ACSI, 2017; UKCSI, 2017). These scores are at the top end of the elite corridor of 80 out of 100 and can be regarded as completing a marathon in just over two hours – it is about as good as it gets.

Who to benchmark against

The first and obvious benchmarks to look for are within your own company. Comparing customer satisfaction scores between different strategic business units, different product groups, operations in different countries and in different segments, will give an indication of where the best and worst performance is being achieved. Scores from previous years will show if there has been an improvement or decline in satisfaction ratings.

Internal benchmarking can be sensitive. It results in league tables, which may imply one part of the company is better than another. Take for example a chemical company with different business units selling speciality chemicals through to commodity chemicals. The speciality chemical unit, which serves a narrow group of customers and provides high levels of technical service, will most probably achieve higher customer satisfaction scores than a division that sells commodity chemicals. The internal benchmarking should not imply that the commodity team is doing a worse job than those selling speciality chemicals; they are operating in a different environment. The internal league table of satisfaction scores will almost certainly create healthy competition between the business units. However, it should not be seen as a stick to beat people with, otherwise it won't be long before clever minds find a way to discredit the use of such metrics and the customer experience programme will fall apart.

Regional differences can also spark arguments within companies. It is not unusual for satisfaction scores to be lower in northern European countries and high in Latin American countries (Wilcock, 2015). This is not necessarily due to the performance of the sales teams, who may be doing an excellent job in the different geographies; rather it could be the result of the more generous disposition of respondents in certain countries. We will talk more about regional differences in the next section in this chapter.

The most obvious benchmarks are those against the competition. Within a set of competitors selling similar products and services there can be a wide range of customer satisfaction scores. If the customer satisfaction scores range wide and fall between 7.0 and 9.0, those with the leading customer satisfaction scores will almost certainly be winning market share and those at the bottom end will be losing. In most business to business markets the customer satisfaction scores of competing companies are closely matched. Most business to business companies have average customer satisfaction scores of between 7.5 and 8.5 out of 10.

In a tracking study, where the customer satisfaction scores are measured at intervals of months or years, we can expect some fluctuations. If the scores are being measured on a scale from 1 to 10, a shift of 0.1 could be an anomaly. If the score changes by a factor of 0.2, this becomes more significant. The number of respondents providing these scores must be taken into consideration. In business to business markets, samples can be quite small and when there are less than 30 to 50 respondents in a survey, we can expect a greater fluctuation in the satisfaction scores between waves than if the sample size comprises 200 or more respondents.

Beyond the direct competitors there is another group of companies that provide interesting benchmarks. These are the companies that are used by a customer but which supply different products and services. Even though they do not compete within the same space, they provide reference points against which all companies are judged. A survey aimed at customers could ask which suppliers the customer uses are considered a standard to be equalled or exceeded. Obtaining a satisfaction score on a scale from 1 to 10 on these paragons will set an aspirational benchmark.

Numeric scores are important in assessing the degree to which excellent customer experiences are achieved. However, like all measures they answer the questions what, where and when and not the questions why or how. After each answer to the ratings score it is important to ask 'why did you say that?' Answers to this question will provide insights that lead to improvements.

Cultural differences

Nationalities respond in different ways to surveys. Some countries are culturally inclined to agree positively with survey questions. This is called positive acquiescence. Also, some people have no problem awarding high scores or low scores on the rating scale while others tend to be more moderate in their responses. We are all capable of giving different scores depending on how we feel on a particular day. It is why we need a significant number of responses in order to accommodate the natural variability that takes place around questions of this type.

Figure 6.1 Response to customer satisfaction questions around the world

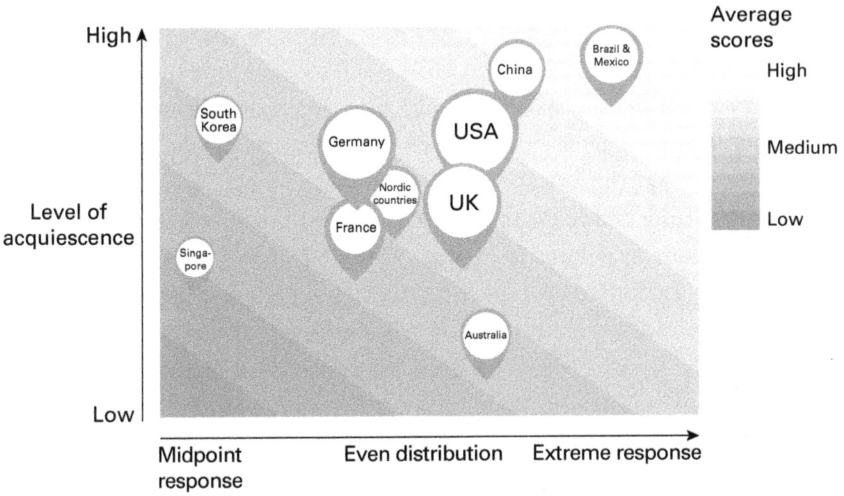

Conor Wilcock, a director at B2B International, analysed customer satisfaction scores from around the world and found that respondents in some countries gave scores that were bunched close together and in other countries respondents spread their satisfaction scores wide across the 10-point scale. When he plotted the degree of acquiescence against the distribution of the responses, he found significant differences between countries (Wilcock, 2017). See Figure 6.1.

There is a strong tendency to acquiesce and agree positively with customer satisfaction questions in Latin American countries, primarily Brazil and Mexico. In Southeast Asia there is similarly a tendency to acquiesce and agree positively with statements although respondents are less inclined to award scores that are quite as high as in Latin America. In contrast, northern European countries and Australia show little tendency to acquiesce and agree positively. The average satisfaction scores in these countries tend to be lower than elsewhere even though respondents may feel their suppliers are doing a great job.

Numeric scales are the safest option when measuring customer experience. Word-based scales using terms such as 'quite satisfied' or 'fairly satisfied' leave room for misinterpretation when they are translated. People throughout the world are used to a 1 to 10 scale where 10 specifies the highest level of satisfaction.

Although we can generalize about the predispositions of different cultures to give different scores to questions on customer experience, it is difficult and unwise to attempt to normalize these by some sort of weighting factor, especially in business to business markets. Many of the audiences in business to business markets are global in their attitudes and subject to Western influence. The degree to which this is the case makes it difficult to second-guess what the variation will be from the norm. In any case, what is the norm? Understanding that the Dutch give lower scores on customer satisfaction than Brazilians is at least helpful in interpreting what might appear to be very different levels of customer experience, but it is not easy to say by how much there is a difference. This means that the safest advice is to always use the raw scores for each country and not attempt to compare them with other countries. What matters within a country is whether the satisfaction score moves up or down rather than how it compares with a score from another region.

Making sense of internal measures isn't always easy. Here is what one contributor to the book said:

'We look at internal measures but not in a homogeneous way. We used to have different ways of measuring customer experience across every country in Europe. The centralized approach we use now is quite new. For example, one of my projects was to measure our deliveries. In some countries we measured satisfaction on deliveries with a question using a 5-point scale, in others we used a 10-point scale or even a semantic scale. Even the way we worded the questions was different. We now use a consistent measure across Europe. On that measure we have 95 per cent consistent delivery of OTIF (on time in full).

We also measure complaints but we haven't yet made this consistent. For example, does everyone log a complaint that the drums were dirty or the product was off spec? We need to harmonize these KPIs.

And then we have different ways of carrying out customer satisfaction surveys across Europe. Some people in the company do it every year, some every two years, some are doing it themselves and some are using outside suppliers. We need to pull all these KPIs together. If we don't have consistency in the way we measure things it leads to arguments and chaos when the results are shared within the company'.

Frequency of measurement

Such is the interest in customer experience measurement, there is a temp-tation to obtain a performance score after every customer interaction. However, customers can be over-dosed with surveys of this kind. If posed too often they will be ignored. As frequent flyers with United Airlines we receive a feedback form after each flight. If others are like us, they will quickly learn to ignore the requests unless they have had a bad experience, in which case the survey will turn into a complaints sheet.

Customer satisfaction surveys once a year are the norm. A 12-month gap between surveys allows for a balanced view of a company's perfor-mance. Even if a recent event sticks in the mind, there is a good chance that a respondent will give a more even-handed view if they are asked to look back over the last 12 months. Most customers accept the legitimacy of customer satisfaction questions being posed on an annual basis. They also will hope that surveys of customer experience lead to improvements from their suppliers and justify the 10 to 15 minutes spent once a year completing the satisfaction survey.

Things to think about

- Which organizations are your company compared against when judging the customer experience you provide?
- What is the gap between the customer experience your company delivers and that of the companies against which it competes?
- What is the gap between the customer experience your company deliv-ers and the standard-bearers in other sectors against which you are compared?
- How do customer experience metrics vary across different parts of your company? What are the reasons for this variability? In what way could you harmonize the measures of customer experience?
- What does the variability of the scores across your company mean? Are they real differences or can they be explained by cultural factors?

References

ACSI (2017) Benchmarks by Industry [Online] available from: www.theacsi.org/ [last accessed 3 October 2017]

UKCSI (2017) The state of customer satisfaction in the UK, July 2017 [Online] available from: www.instituteofcustomerservice.com/ [last accessed 3 October 2017]

Wilcock, C (2015) Accounting for Cultural Bias in B2B Research, *Research Live*, 12 August 2015 [Online] available from: https://www.research-live.com/article/features/accounting-for-cultural-bias-in-b2b-research/id/4013742 [last accessed 3 October 2017]

Wilcock, C (2017) Comparing Apples to Pommes: Understanding and Accounting for Cultural Bias in Global B2B Research [Online] available from: www.b2binternational.com/publications/understanding-accounting-cultural-bias-global-b2b-research/ [last accessed 3 October 2017]

What are the key drivers of customer experience? 07

Memory as a driver of CX

We can choose to remember certain things such as what we need to know in order to pass an exam. These memories require hard work and constant repetition of a subject until it finally sticks. Other things stay in our memory for a long time because something extraordinary happens that spikes individual neurons and encodes the event. Events that are routine or inconsequential are unlikely to linger long. There is nothing of note to fix them in our minds. Our memories are affected by stimuli. We particularly remember the good times and the bad.

The implications of this are important for customer experience programmes. When something goes badly wrong for a customer it almost certainly will be remembered and in a negative way. A failure in customer experience is likely to induce emotional rather than physical pain. Studies show that emotional pain is remembered much longer (Winch, 2014). It may be possible to recover from a disastrous customer experience with its emotional consequences although it goes without saying that a major problem will need a big and possibly delicate recovery.

Fortunately, outstanding customer experience is also remembered. If a supplier gets a customer out of trouble with a super quick delivery of product or technical advice that solves a problem, the event will be seared into the memory by neurons. It is why we can recall, as if it were yesterday, the time our car broke down on that wet, dark winter evening and the breakdown recovery company sorted out our problem.

Solving a customer's problem will always be more memorable than delivering outstanding customer service. There may be ways in which the experience can be made more memorable. Breaking the customer experience event into episodes can help. People find it easier to think through episodes of an experience rather like scenes in a film. If the event is accompanied by things that trigger the senses, it may provide additional memory cues.

At the start of a workshop we like to ask people to share their stories about companies they think do a great job at delivering customer experience. This is a test of the degree to which customer experience events stay in the memory. A number of common themes are mentioned. Occasionally people will talk about a product that has wowed them. Sometimes it will be novel technology. Most of the stories involve service of one kind or another. This is never a surprise. Over the years we have built up a picture of what drives great customer experience and we know that people are usually involved. Here is a list of the experiences that people say are most memorable:

- **Be responsive:** the most frequently mentioned reason for excellent customer service is responsiveness. Customers want immediate responses to their enquiries. They want quick deliveries. They ask for instant solutions. We are a time-hungry world.

- **Listen and learn:** companies that listen to their customers' feedback and take it on board are rated highly in delivering excellent customer experience.

- **Be friendly:** there is nothing like a smile and a dose of enthusiasm for creating excellent customer experience.

- **Show respect:** customers are important and they know it. Companies delivering excellent customer experience show an appropriate amount of respect and appreciation.

- **Communicate:** customers expect and want communications from their suppliers. In particular they want relevant communications about their orders, new products or things that will interest them.

- **Great products:** people love to tell others about novel, innovative, good quality and well-designed products. The product is, after all, at the heart of any purchase.

- **Know your product and service:** customers are impressed if a supplier can demonstrate knowledge of them and their needs. They expect suppliers to know their own portfolio of products and services. They want to communicate with someone who can show how these products and services will match the customers' needs.

- **Manage and beat expectations**: customers want to know what is going to happen and then make sure that it does, if possible beating the promise they have been given. Beating customers' expectations wins considerable appreciation.

- **Say thank you**: these two small words have a big influence on customers. Saying thank you shows appreciation and recognition of the value you place on their business.

- **Patience**: delivering excellent customer experience takes time and energy to get right. It is a marathon and not a sprint.

- **Aim for perfection**: it is not good enough to be okay. Almost every supplier is at this level otherwise they wouldn't be in business. Companies that excel at customer experience aim not just for okay but for 'wow' – to make their service memorable in a positive way.

- **Trained staff**: everyone working at a supplier that is in touch with customers is a potential ambassador. They need careful selection so they have the right abilities and attitude. They need the right training so they can deliver an unforgettable excellent experience.

Using science to determine the drivers of customer experience

If you have enjoyed a wonderful meal with great service at a restaurant, you may rise from the table and use effusive words to describe it. It is just possible, but unlikely, that you could simply say 'that meal gets 9 out of 10'. This is how market researchers ask questions. They like to use measures wherever they can. Words give insights but they do not provide firm anchors. Numbers put a peg in the ground so it is possible to compare the customer experience with other parts of the company or other companies and to track the trends over time.

The scales that are used for measuring customer experience have to be big enough to allow discrimination. A simple three-point scale of good, neutral and bad would be too narrow to communicate a range of feelings. On the other hand, a scale from 1 to 100 could be too broad. Researchers have settled on scales from 1 to 10 as an acceptable measure for customer experience and satisfaction.

Think back to the example of enquiring about satisfaction with a meal at a restaurant. Let's assume that someone gives a score of 9 out of 10 – the meal

Table 7.1 Satisfaction scores given to individual attributes of the restaurant experience

Attribute measured	Score out of 10
Quality of the food	7
Amount of food	6
Presentation of the food	7
Ambience of the restaurant	8
Attentiveness of the waiter	10
Friendliness of the waiter	10
Ease of booking the table	5
Value for money	8

was very much enjoyed. We would normally ask why they attributed this score and the answer should provide additional insights. We are, however, dependent on people's ability to describe and explain. In an attempt to find out exactly why the meal was enjoyed, additional rating questions could be asked to find out what was thought of the food, the ambience of the restaurant and so on. Again using a scale from 1 to 10 we could get a result such as that shown in Table 7.1.

Now let us imagine that we ask 20 or more people the same questions. The responses will not be exactly the same but there are likely to be some similarities. If one of these similarities was that a high overall satisfaction score was also accompanied by a high score for the friendliness of the waiter, we can determine that the two scores are intrinsically linked. In statistical terms we refer to this link as a correlation coefficient. A correlation coefficient of 1.0 indicates a perfect link between factors. It would be unusual to get such a strong association but any score of 0.5 or more indicates a positive correlation and one that enables us to see that it is a factor that drives satisfaction.

Table 7.2 shows the correlations between an overall satisfaction score, and the satisfaction scores given to individual components of the offer, of 500 customers of a large metals company.

What we see from the analysis is that, in the case of the metals company, the customer experience is very much driven by helping customers achieve their goals, being trustworthy and being easy to do business with.

This analysis is interesting but it doesn't tell the metals company whether it is performing well or badly on the different attributes. A separate

Table 7.2 Correlation between overall satisfaction and satisfaction with specific elements of a metals supplier's offer

Attribute on which satisfaction was measured	Correlation with overall satisfaction
Helps me achieve the goals of my company	0.76
Is a company I can trust	0.72
Is easy to do business with	0.69
Provides my company with effective solutions	0.64
Works hard to earn and retain my business	0.59
Has representatives that are responsive	0.56
Understands my business	0.53
Has competitive prices	0.50
Offers deliveries within an acceptable lead time	0.44
Delivers consistent product performance and quality	0.43
Has knowledgeable representatives	0.42
Is committed to environmental and social principles	0.41
Is a technology and innovation leader	0.37
Has a portfolio of products that meets my needs	0.32

question asked respondents to what extent they thought the metals company was better or worse than the competition on each of the attributes. Table 7.3 shows that on some of the attributes that are strong drivers of satisfaction (helping the customer achieve their goals, easy to do business with, providing effective solutions etc), the company was not considered to be particularly strong, relative to competitors. This provided pointers as to where improvements were required. The sales team, who always felt to be short of new products, could see that increasing the product portfolio would have little impact on overall satisfaction. The rather surprising low correlation between product quality and overall satisfaction was not because it is unimportant but product quality was already very good and other things had risen as priorities that drive satisfaction.

Although this example is specific to the metal industry, it illustrates a principle that can be observed across hundreds of business to business customer experience surveys. It is the softer factors in the customer value propositions that deliver great customer experience rather than the more tangible factors such as product quality, product range, delivery and price.

Table 7.3   Correlation with overall satisfaction and satisfaction levels on individual attributes

Attribute on which satisfaction was measured	Correlation with overall satisfaction	% saying company is better than the competition
Helps me achieve the goals of my company	0.76	21%
Is a company I can trust	0.72	48%
Is easy to do business with	0.69	19%
Provides my company with effective solutions	0.64	15%
Works hard to earn and retain my business	0.59	16%
Has representatives that are responsive	0.56	19%
Understands my business	0.53	33%
Has competitive prices	0.50	35%
Offers deliveries within an acceptable lead time	0.44	34%
Delivers consistent product performance and quality	0.43	70%
Has knowledgeable representatives	0.42	38%
Is committed to environmental and social principles	0.41	29%
Is a technology and innovation leader	0.37	14%
Has a portfolio of products that meets my needs	0.32	46%

A company needs to perform well on these tangible factors, otherwise they wouldn't even be considered as a supplier. They are the table stakes that are required to do business. On the basis that all the table stakes have been met by every supplier and therefore are very similar, it is the softer factors that rise in importance and are most appreciated.

Significantly, many of the softer factors do not require massive investments. Helping a company achieve its goals does not require a bigger sales team. It does require the sales team to listen and respond imaginatively with suggestions as to how they can help customers grow. It requires the vendor to not just sell products but to offer ideas, solutions and a partnership. These may not necessarily be costly in capital investment but they are not easy offers to pick off the shelf. A special calibre of salesperson is needed to use the products that are on offer to help a customer achieve its goals. Sometimes this could involve recommending that the customer switches to another product that is better suited to their needs (and may save them money) and sometimes it may mean thinking outside the box and recommending a new way of doing business.

The importance of being 'easy to do business with' confirms the relevance of the customer effort score. Time-hungry people don't want to spend their scarce resource chasing suppliers. Ease of doing business with Amazon is one of the reasons it scores so highly in terms of customer satisfaction.

Ease of doing business means different things in different businesses. In the case of Amazon they make it easy to order and easy to pay. In business to business markets, ease of doing business may mean having sufficient people on the customer service desk so that phones are answered straight away. It may mean that the sales representatives can make decisions themselves without having to refer them back to head office. It may mean minimizing the paperwork and bureaucracy so often involved in on-boarding a new customer. It may mean that customers value salespeople who are knowledgeable about the product range and able to solve their problems by suggesting alternatives if something is out of stock.

The importance of emotions

At various stages in the book we talk about the importance of emotions. This chapter is about the drivers of customer experience and we know that emotions are important in driving high satisfaction scores. When we ask somebody why they say that a customer experience is good they are likely to provide a rational answer:

'They always have products in stock.'
'Their prices are the best in the market.'
'They are amazing because they deliver their products next day.'

These answers may be logical and correct but they may not reflect the real reason for attributing a high score to the customer experience. A company that is perfect in how it executes its offer may not be liked. A strong emotional bond is an important driver of feelings of customer experience.

The feelings that we have for a company will usually have been built up over time in small increments. Friendly staff will be sure to have some effect. The consistency of the way they deal with the customer and present their offer will create trust and build a sense of security.

Now let's imagine that something changes at a supplier. The company may change its name or there is a change in customer-facing staff. The name change of the company in itself may not matter but it could raise concerns as to whether the company has been taken over or is recreating itself in a new paradigm. A change in staff could raise concerns that the new people won't understand all the nuances in the customers' needs. The changes may ultimately be for the better but only time will show this to be the case. In the meantime, customers may fear that the new status quo could destabilize a good working relationship and this will raise emotional concerns.

Customers cannot always distinguish between the emotional and rational elements of their decisions. They tend to overrate the influence of the rational component. When asked the reasons a supplier is chosen the usual responses are logical, such as great product quality, good delivery, excellent prices, value for money and so on. Very few would say their choice is strongly influenced by the brand. And yet, when we ask companies how long they have used their suppliers it is not unusual to learn that is 'for many years'. It is inconceivable that over many years no other company has offered improved products, delivery or prices and yet people are inclined to continue buying from the same suppliers. This may be because there is a fear that other suppliers will be no better or genuine attachment to the existing supplier and the people that work within it. Emotional factors usually trump rational factors when it comes to supplier choice.

We know that in other areas of our lives emotions have a huge effect, for example in influencing the choice of partner that we decide to live with for the rest of our lives. The choice of company we select to do business with is subject to the same emotions. We do business with people we like doing business with. This shouldn't be a surprise, but it is often ignored.

Scientists are still trying to figure out how the brain works. The human brain is divided into two hemispheres – left and right. Current belief is that the left-hand side of the brain controls most of our logical thinking while our emotions are determined by the functions of the right-hand side. We need to address both sides of the brain in our attempts to deliver

Figure 7.1   The rational and emotional sections of the brain and their influence on experiences

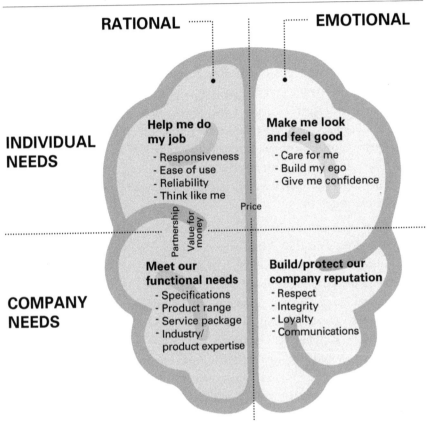

RATIONAL   EMOTIONAL

INDIVIDUAL NEEDS

Help me do my job
- Responsiveness
- Ease of use
- Reliability
- Think like me

Make me look and feel good
- Care for me
- Build my ego
- Give me confidence

Price

Partnership   Value for money

COMPANY NEEDS

Meet our functional needs
- Specifications
- Product range
- Service package
- Industry/ product expertise

Build/protect our company reputation
- Respect
- Integrity
- Loyalty
- Communications

SOURCE Used with permission from B2B International

better customer experience. The left-hand side of the brain, the part that determines logical and rational thought, will be impressed by the way we can help the customer do their job. If we can demonstrate that we are responsive, easy to work with and reliable, it will resonate. The left-hand side of the brain will also gain much satisfaction from our product specifications, the product range and the service packages that we provide. See Figure 7.1.

It is at the right-hand side of the brain where the emotions kick in. Here we must work on emotions in the same way we would if we were dealing with a loved one in our private life. Let us examine what is happening at the right-hand side of the brain and illustrated in Figure 7.1.

Meeting individual needs

The buyer or specifier at the customer company wants to look good in front of colleagues. A business to business supplier can help in this regard by the following:

Care for me: individuals within a company must feel that they are cared for. They want to feel that they will be helped whenever needed. Occasionally customers make a mistake by placing the wrong order and the supplier has the opportunity to save the day. If the problem for the customer is solved without fuss or blame they will forever be grateful. If the customer is looked after with a treat every now and then, they will be made to feel special. Customers are people and it is human instinct to want to be cared for.

Build my ego: people want to look good in the eyes of their peers. If a supplier does something that benefits a customer, the person or people that chose that supplier will be bathed in reflected glory. Equally those people who chose the supplier do not want to be blamed if the supplier fails in some way. Great customer experience makes sure that the decision makers who chose the supplier are always credited with the supplier's triumphs. A supplier that makes a concession so the customer gets a better deal should celebrate with the customer their success in achieving it. For example, a supplier whose just-in-time deliveries free up warehouse space for the customer should let the customer have the credit for this new and valuable resource even though the hard work and the solution wasn't their idea.

Give me confidence: individuals who place an order with a supplier are vesting a huge amount of trust in its ability to fulfil its promises. A supplier that consistently does what it says it will do allows customers to sleep soundly at night.

Meeting company needs

Just as the individuals at the customer company have emotional needs, so does the organization. The organization relies on its suppliers to maintain its image in the marketplace. This means companies demand the following from their suppliers:

Respect: companies have a choice as to which suppliers they use and they like to use those that are respected. It is why computer companies like to advertise 'Intel Inside' or garment manufacturers advertise that their wet-weather gear is made from Gore-Tex. These are respected supplier brands and their positive qualities will be conferred to the companies that use them in their finished products.

Integrity: companies, like people, want to deal with suppliers with certain credentials. Honesty and integrity are, of course important. Increasingly, so are certifications and green credentials. Suppliers need to be able to demonstrate that they can meet these standards.

Loyalty: customers want to know that their suppliers are committed to their industry. They want to know that their suppliers are not fly-by-nights that are out to make a quick buck while the market is buoyant. They know that markets are cyclical and they want to know their suppliers will be there in good times and bad.

Communications: a supplier of business to business products will win approval if they help promote their customers' products or services. This may be something as simple as listing distributors where the products can be purchased through to making a contribution to a customer's advertising campaign. Although this may generate strong positive emotions, we can also see that these may last only as long as the generous contribution to the customer's advertising continues!

Employees as drivers of excellent customer experience

James Heskett, a professor at Harvard University, understood the importance of employees in delivering excellent customer experience. His thesis, *The Service Profit Chain* (Heskett *et al*, 1997), is based on the belief that happy staff deliver better service and better service builds custom, which in turn builds profits. His point is obvious and we see evidence of it every day. Airlines in disputes with their employees about pay and conditions usually receive poor customer satisfaction scores because the staff are resentful. Retailers with contented employees create a culture of happiness in the stores and delight customers. These are very public manifestations of how employees can drive excellent customer experience.

In business to business markets the interactions between employees and customers are just as great. Customers speak regularly to customer service desks and appreciate a personalized service. They like contact with knowledgeable and helpful sales representatives. They want to be recognized by name when they call. They like to deal with the same people who know their requirements and feel concerned when changes are made. Technical service teams, credit controllers, and dispatchers are all important points of contact. They may well perform their functional tasks very well indeed but they may not understand the role they play in delivering excellent customer experience.

When printers order paper from a paper merchant, they expect deliveries quickly, usually the next day. Paper merchants deliver to customers two or three times a week. This means that the van driver has more face-to-face contact with customers than any other person at the paper merchant. A paper merchant had a Damascene moment when he realized the importance of van drivers as unsung heroes. The role of the van drivers was elevated. Vans were given fresh livery and kept clean. Drivers were given a smart uniform and trained as customer service emissaries. Drivers learned the names of the printers they serviced and built a friendly rapport. They helped move deliveries of paper into customers' premises including loading it on to the printing machines if asked. These changes cost little and had a massive positive influence on the perceptions of customer experience provided by the paper merchant.

Things to think about

- Do you know the factors that are driving your customers' views on excellent customer experience?
- What do you do to make things positively memorable for customers?
- How good is your company at helping customers achieve their goals?
- How good is your company in being easy to do business with?
- What is the emotional intelligence of your company?
- To what extent does your company understand and manage emotions in building good customer experience?
- How far through your company does the emotional connection with customers exist?

References

Heskett, JL, Sasser, E and Schlesinger, LA (1997) *The Service Profit Chain: How leading companies link profit and growth to loyalty, satisfaction, and value*, The Free Press, New York

Winch, G (2014) 5 Ways Emotional Pain is Worse Than Physical Pain [Online] available from: www.psychologytoday.com/blog/the-squeaky-wheel/201407/5-ways-emotional-pain-is-worse-physical-pain [last accessed 3 October 2017]

Customer journey mapping and how to apply it

08

The customer journey

Whenever a customer (or potential customer) interacts with a company, visually, verbally or physically, there is a touch point. These touch points may be simple interactions. It may be someone noticing a suppliers' truck, it could be the receipt of an email, it may be a phone call from a company. Each touch point contributes in some small way to shaping the view of a company and in this respect it influences customers' experiences. There may be dozens of such interactions at different points on the customer journey. If a supplier hasn't thought through the implications of these touch points, they could generate negative feelings. Equally there could be some touch points where, without realizing it, a company excels and has a strong competitive advantage that could be exploited. Managing the customer journey therefore plays an important role in delivering excellent customer experience.

We should think of the customer journey as a sort of life-cycle. Before there are any interactions with a company, customers acquire knowledge. This is the birth of the journey. The build-up of awareness and knowledge can take place over a protracted period. Adverts, promotions and PR feed messages to customers and potential customers. In business to business marketing, word-of-mouth, personal recommendations, visits to exhibitions and seminars can all play a part in building up a picture of a supplier.

Research carried out by Google tells us that 71 per cent of B2B buyers use the internet to search for information prior to contacting a supplier (Lecinski, 2011). In fact, the research says that the general public and business to business buyers act very much the same, using the internet to search for background data on a company or product before engaging with the company directly. This digital connection takes place right at the beginning of the customer journey and has given rise to the term *zero moment of truth* (ZMOT). It is an important point as it affects the role of the business to business representative. In the past many questions that a potential customer had about a company's products and services were answered by sales reps. Today business to business customers know a great deal about the products they are interested in buying before they contact the supplier. This means that the only questions they may have for the supplier are 'How much does it cost?', 'When can I have it delivered?' A customer service desk can provide this information over the telephone. The role of the sales rep is therefore changing and becoming a technical adviser, problem solver or solutions supplier.

At this early point in the customer journey there is little or no relationship with a company as business has yet to be transacted. Using the internet the potential customer can dig deep into the company's product portfolio, its product specifications, its support services, its prices – all the components of its customer value proposition. In addition, the customer may canvass the opinion of friends and colleagues to see what they know about the company.

As the engagement between the customer and the company develops, the interest in doing business may get to the point where terms and conditions are discussed, negotiations take place, and trial orders are placed. Because we are talking about a new relationship, there could be some slips and trips on the way. How these are dealt with will have an influence on the success of the business partnership.

If things go well regular business transactions will take place with the company. This will involve placing orders, receiving deliveries and dealing with the inevitable problems that occasionally occur in any supply chain.

There is no reason why the relationship should not continue successfully for years. In many business to business customer/supplier relationships, companies manage their ups and downs just as two people manage their marital relationships. Sometimes the relationship gets broken for one reason or another and the customer leaves the supplier.

We have referred to the two parties in this arrangement as the customer and the supplier. Of course, this is not impersonal. People are involved and there could be a number of them. The initial dealings between the customer and the supplier may be with members of the customer's technical team who are interested in the technical properties of the products. There could also be some high-level influence at board level with members of the leadership team favouring companies from a certain geographical region or that are part of their extended group. Procurement staff are nearly always involved at some stage.

The supplier in turn has a variety of players who have different interests at different stages. Early on in the relationship the supplier's technical team may converse with the customer's technical team. When the customer comes on board and deliveries begin, the supply chain staff and the customer service people will communicate regularly with the customer. Throughout the process there is likely to be a salesperson or account executive who coordinates proceedings.

The involvement of these participants at the customer and the supplier creates an elaborate mix of relationships at different stages in the journey. Through examining the customer journey we see that there are opportunities for multiple customer experiences depending on who is involved and at what stage they take place in the relationship.

These customer experiences are sometimes referred to as 'moments of truth'. This phrase was popularized in a book entitled *Moments of Truth* by Jan Carlzon (Carlzon, 1987), which we mentioned in Chapter 2. The impressive point about Carlzon and the story of Scandinavian Airlines is that he turned the company around, not by cutting costs, not by making changes to its prices, but by empowering his staff so they could understand and deal with customers' needs quickly and efficiently. A year after Carlzon took over, SAS became the most punctual airline in Europe; losses were turned into a profit of $54 million in 1982.

Mapping the journey

As Carlzon's actions show us, the customer journey can be mapped. Like any map, it can be at a high level or in considerable detail. At the highest level it can be broken into half a dozen or more major stages (see Figure 8.1). These stages create the spine of the map and broadly follow the AIDA communications model (awareness, leads to interest and, if things go well for the company generates desire and action – hence AIDA). Beyond the four steps of the AIDA model there could be other milestones such as complaints, leaving the company, returning, etc. There is no hard and fast structure for these major stages; they must be developed, as appropriate, for the customer–supplier relationship that is being examined.

Hanging underneath the major headings on the spine are all the moments of truth that occur within that stage of the journey. Each of these moments of truth can be assessed in terms of its importance to the customer and whether they are strengths or weaknesses of the supplier.

Figure 8.1 High-level customer journey map

AWARENESS	INTEREST	DECISION	SERVICE SET-UP	SERVICE DELIVERY	RELATIONSHIP STRENGTHENING	CONCERN	LEAVE	RETURN
How customers become aware of Company X	How customers become interested in doing business with Company X	The things that help customers make the decision to do business with Company X	What Company X does when setting-up a new customer account	The day-to-day elements involved in the delivery of the agreed service	What Company X does to develop on-going relationships and delight its customers	How Company X deals with concerns and complaints	What Company X does when a customer wants to leave	How we win back previous customers
Trucks/Livery	Prospect material	Proposal/presentation	Customer site visit	Phone/fax/email for order	Additional product installs	Receiving complaints	Leaving phone call	Prospects lists
Brands-portfolio	Promotional offers	Face-to-face visits	Customer site assessment	Customer places order	Customer training	Following up complaints	Stop ordering altogether	AM contact plan
Brand-umbrella/corporate	One-stop-shop offer	Agreement	Welcome call	Customer places order - phone call	Business Dev. Manager	Price rise letter	Visit	Lapsed customer call
CSR	Existing product lines	Can't service/notify of rejection	Account creation	Product delivery	Free service extras	Standard AM calls	Last chance visit	
Word of mouth	Lending		Face-to-face rep visits	Customer service calls	Loans/commercial manager			
Site/Plant visibility	Brand's literature				Promotional support			
Prospecting					AM phone call			
Charity involvement					Customer audit			
Social media					Face-to-face visit			
					Favourable credit/increase limit			

Moments of truth

- Critically important
- Extremely important
- Very important
- Important

SOURCE Used with permission from B2B International

Just as a traveller would keep referring to a map as they negotiate a journey, so too it is good to keep the journey map visible within the company that has created it. Customer journey maps make great wall charts, attract considerable attention and generate lots of healthy discussion. If they are to be converted into a wall poster, there may be some physical limits as to what can be marked on the map at each stage. Different customer journey maps should be prepared for each customer segment served by a company. Variations of these customer journey maps could include:

- All the moments of truth classified according to their perceived importance to customers.
- The strengths and weaknesses of the company with each of the moments of truth.
- The customer who is a target at a particular stage.
- Key competitors at a particular stage.
- The emotions of customers at a particular stage.
- Actions that are required to improve performance at a particular stage.

How to develop customer journey maps

The initial customer journey map usually begins in a workshop where brainstorming generates ideas for the stages of the spine and the moments of truth within each stage. It may seem strange to create this first cut of the map internally but that is because people within a company are able to have a view across the whole life-cycle, whereas customers only see a part of it depending on where they are in that life-cycle. Customers will have a chance to have their say, but this comes later when the map is validated.

It makes sense for the workshop participants to represent the different functions in the company. As we will see, it is the flawless interconnections between these different silos of a company that ensure a great experience for customers.

The mapping begins with the workshop facilitator arriving at an agreement as to a segment of customers that will be the focus of the journey map. The major stages that form the spine are decided and then begins the detail of listing all the touch points (moments of truth) that form each stage of the spine.

Customer touch points are not the preserve of sales and marketing staff. Customers may touch financial staff, technical staff, delivery staff, receptionists and the like. This is another good reason for having a broad range of

Table 8.1 Steps in developing a customer journey map (CJM)

Step 1	Agree on segment that will be addressed in the customer journey	Decide which group of customers will be addressed. The customer journey should be run for a specific segment.
Step 2	Invite to workshop	Invite up to 20 people to workshop. The workshop will probably require half a day. Attendees should be anyone who impacts upon customer experience, ie, not just people in marketing and sales.
Step 3	Kicking off the workshop	A moderator will lead the workshop by introducing the concept of the customer journey and moments of truth. They will explain the process and outcomes.
Step 4	Setting the spine	The starting point is the journey spine – the major events of the customer journey. These parts of the spine are likely to broadly follow the AIDA model – awareness, interest, desire, action. Added to which there will be spinal stages such as complaints and exit/lost customers. Workshop participants must agree on the spine. Flipcharts are marked up with the labels of the spine.
Step 5	Groups work on parts of the spine	The workshop breaks into groups, each group allocated a segment. The groups brainstorm and list on Post-It notes all moments of truth (MOT) on that part of the spine. These MOT are physical interventions with the customer. Each MOT should be marked as to whether it is a pain point or pleasure point. The Post-It notes are ranked in order of importance on the flipchart.
Step 6	Groups review each others' work	Each group feeds back its MOT for the different parts of the spine to the plenary workshop. In plenary, adjustments are made to the importance of the MOT, pain points or pleasure points. Missing MOT may be added. Agreement on the CJM is required as the meeting closes.
Step 7	Customer journey map is created in Excel	Following the workshop the moderators enter the MOT into Excel. The Excel charts are circulated to the attendees of the workshop for their approval.
Step 8	Validation	Last (and not least) the CJM is validated with customers. Usually this is in depth (qualitatively) to ensure everything has been covered by the workshop.

participants in the workshop. It is good to have representation from anyone who may directly or indirectly affect the customers' experience with the company. Even if people within the various company departments don't personally interact with customers, their actions and internal processes will almost certainly affect customers in some way.

A suggested process for creating the customer journey maps at the workshop is shown in Table 8.1.

Speaking to customers

The development of the customer journey map is a cathartic process. Very often the workshop concludes with a map and a list of action points. As people come together from different parts of the company to think how they can deliver a better customer experience, there are many wake-up calls as to what could be done to make the process better. The internal focus provides insights and helps join the silos of the company.

The internal view needs external validation by customers. It is easy for customers to skip points in the journey, which get taken for granted and may not be mentioned at the time of the interview. We need a method of interviewing that unlocks the customer's mind for the whole journey. A qualitative market research project among a couple of dozen customers may be sufficient. The aim of these interviews is to establish if the sequence of events is correct, that the moments of truth have all been identified and they have the right classification in terms of importance, delight or pain point.

Depth interviews allow respondents 'dwell time' during which they can think about the steps of the journey. The beginning of the journey will be somewhere around the time that the respondent became aware of a new supplier or decided that it was time to seek one out. From that starting point the researcher is interested in each customer's story, working out how they moved through the journey until eventually becoming a regular customer.

It can be helpful to treat the journey as a movie, made up of episodes. Each episode is a stage in the customer journey. The researcher asks the respondent to think back to where they were when they first started to think about a new supplier. The 'where' question is important. If a respondent can locate where they were at a point in the journey they can readily think about who was with them, what was happening and describe the 'film set'.

The question 'why' may not be asked outright. Of course we are interested in why respondents think and act in a certain way, but a direct question could generate a bias that steers the discussion. For example, if someone is asked early in the journey why they were looking for a new supplier they may provide a rational answer such as 'to get a better price', 'to have a better security of supply', 'to keep the competition on their toes', etc. These rational and logical responses may provide only part of the story as the real reason for looking for a new supplier could be more obtuse. Something could have happened in the relationship with the incumbent supplier that broke the trust, so prompting the search for a new one. Something could have happened within the customer's company such as a senior director saying to the procurement team 'you should have a look at company X, I hear they are a very good supplier.' The question 'why' will eventually be answered through interpreting everything that is described in the episodic interviewing rather than in answer to direct questions.

The aim of the customer research is to validate the customer journey. If customers suggest additional stages or moments of truth, they would be added to the journey.

Equally, the internal workshop may have identified processes within the company that customers don't know about or need to know. For example, processes for checking customers' credit levels or communications between departments required to confirm the smooth settlement of an order. Nevertheless these are still important moments of truth in the journey, even if not visible to the customer.

Communicating the customer journey map

Once verified, the customer journey map can be confirmed. Customer journey maps are not to be folded away in a drawer or hidden in a computer file. They are, as their name suggests, maps to guide the company as it deals with its different customers.

Customer journey maps are great catalysts for conversation. If they are pinned to the wall people stop and look at them. For some people they will provide a new and different way of looking at customer interactions. They will generate conversations and, crucially, they will show the importance of different departments contributing to the journey. The maps become vehicles for breaking down department silos.

If the maps are used as wall posters it is worth considering turning them into infographics. In this way they can be made visually more interesting, emphasizing aspects of the story that will lead to improved customer experience. Using customer journey maps to help communicate improvements in customer experience was described by one of our contributors to the book:

'I've got the customer journey maps plastered all over the wall in my office. I've got lots of ad hoc presentations of them all over the room. We use these maps in as many meetings as possible. We use them to communicate what we are doing in our customer service team. When we are out with our colleagues we don't always refer to it as customer journey mapping. We may refer to it as "ease of doing business". We are a company of 1500 people and everybody plays their part in customer experience. We have to be very approachable as a customer service team. We have to take away all the complexities and make it simple. In essence, we try to keep it simple, sell the benefits, get everyone engaged, and communicate, communicate what we're doing.'

Things to think about

- Who within your organization will spearhead the customer journey mapping initiative? Is it supported at a high level?

- For each segment that you serve, consider developing a customer journey map. How many customer journey maps do you need?

- Do you have access to a moderator with the skills that can bring together different departments to develop the customer journey maps?

- Consider using an external facilitator to run the customer journey mapping sessions.

- Who will attend the CJM workshops?

- Who will carry out the validation of the customer journey maps with customers themselves? Can this work be carried out internally or will it require external help?

- How will the customer journey maps be used when they are validated? How will they be shared around the company?

References

Carlzon, J (1987) *Moments of Truth*, Ballinger Publishing Company, Cambridge MA
Lecinski, J (2011) *ZMOT Winning the Zero Moment of Truth* [Online] e-book, available from: https://www.thinkwithgoogle.com/marketing-resources/micro-moments/2011-winning-zmot-ebook/ [last accessed 5 December 2017]

PART THREE
Strategies for achieving excellent customer experience

Developing a customer experience strategy

09

Pillars of customer experience

Improving customer experience in a business to business company is likely to follow a typical sequence of steps such as those described by PR Smith's SOSTAC® Plan (Smith, 2017). This strategic planning framework is made up of six stages:

S – Situation analysis. This initial stage is an analysis of the level of customer experience provided by the company. This is likely to be based on various metrics such as customer satisfaction scores, the Net Promoter Score® and the customer effort score. These we discussed in Chapter 5. It would also be the point at which customer journey maps are developed for each segment of the market that is served. Through mapping the market, it will highlight any problems and suggest some solutions. See Chapter 8.

O – Objectives. With a full understanding of the problems from the mapping process, objectives can be set for improving customer experience. These we discussed in Chapters 4 and 5.

S – Strategy. A strategy would be worked out for meeting the objectives. These would be high-level factors that need to be in place to make sure that the objectives are met. The strategy is made up of a number of principles or pillars and these are the focus of this chapter.

T – Tactics. These are the detailed things to do to improve customer experience. It is the answering of phones after three rings, it is remembering a customer's birthday, it is dealing with a complaint and offering a resolution with the addition of something special. It is making sure that we focus on the things that drive customer satisfaction, as described in Chapter 7.

Figure 9.1 PR Smith's SOSTAC® model

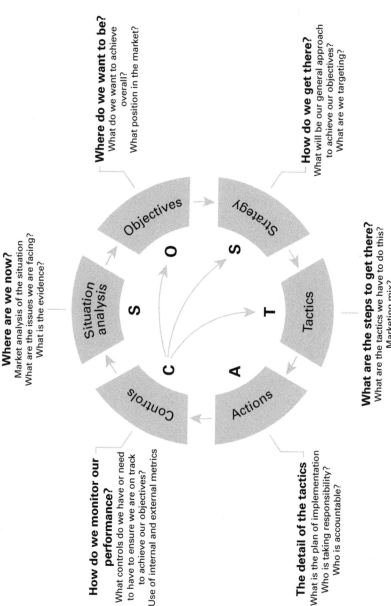

Where are we now?
Market analysis of the situation
What are the issues we are facing?
What is the evidence?

Where do we want to be?
What do we want to achieve overall?
What position in the market?

How do we get there?
What will be our general approach to achieve our objectives?
What are we targeting?

What are the steps to get there?
What are the tactics we have to do this?
Marketing mix?

The detail of the tactics
What is the plan of implementation
Who is taking responsibility?
Who is accountable?

How do we monitor our performance?
What controls do we have or need to have to ensure we are on track to achieve our objectives?
Use of internal and external metrics

Situation analysis
S

Objectives
O

Strategy
S

Tactics
T

Actions
A

Controls
C

SOURCE SOSTAC® is a registered trademark of PR Smith. For more information on SOSTAC® Planning and becoming a SOSTAC® Certified Planner visit www.SOSTAC.org

A – Action. Create an action plan showing who will do what, by when and with what resources. Targets will be set for some of the important metrics such as customer satisfaction and Net Promoter Scores®. We talk about this in detail in Chapters 10, 11 and 12.

C – Control. A control mechanism is built into the plan. If it goes off course there will be an opportunity for corrective action. These controls we discuss further in Chapters 20 and 21.

It is the strategy component of PR Smith's SOSTAC® process that we are interested in in this chapter. Customer experience programmes are supported by six pillars, which we described in Chapter 4. As a reminder they are:

1 commitment;
2 fulfilment;
3 seamlessness;
4 responsiveness;
5 proactivity;
6 evolution.

These pillars set the strategy for a successful customer experience programme in a business to business company. Undoubtedly different companies will place greater or lesser emphasis on one or other of the pillars. As we have already seen, only between a quarter and a half of business to business companies acknowledge that they are performing well on these important components of a customer experience strategy.

Commitment

Only 48 per cent of B2B companies say they perform well on this factor (Cupman, 2016).

People who set out to achieve something, especially something that is going to be difficult and that will take a long time, make a pledge. They promise to themselves and others that they will achieve an objective, that they will not give up and they will see things through. We are not suggesting that everyone who embarks on a customer experience programme should put their hand on their heart, raise their eyes to the heavens and chant some fine words. However, we do believe it is necessary for people leading a customer experience programme to really mean what they say about it being important and that they are committed to making it happen.

This means that if and when there are choices to make, as indeed there will be, the customer experience programme isn't shunted onto the back burner. Customer experience is a strategic initiative and the results will take time to show through, which can make it tempting to push it back if times are difficult.

The cost of a customer experience programme is likely to be relatively small in the overall scheme of things. A lot of the actions for the programme require changes to the company culture and personal attitudes. Although in theory it should be possible to change these at the flick of a switch, in practice changing behaviours is difficult as existing habits and behaviours can be deeply ingrained.

The commitment for the programme has to come from someone who is in a position to make things happen. Ideally this should be the CEO but it could be any leader of a team who is prepared to stick their neck out to make a difference.

CEOs are understandably driven by financial justifications. Most want to see evidence of a financial return as is evidenced by one of our contributors.

'We began our customer experience programme in the UK. It proved highly successful and got other parts of our company interested. When Canada started on their journey they wanted to know what the ROI would be. Our recommendation was to feel the fear and do it anyway. We were able to share with Canada our return on investment which was very healthy indeed. We suggested that they could expect to see the same sort of result. But you never know, maybe Canada could see an even bigger effect. But you've got to have top level buy-in.'

A success story will carry weight within a company if it can be supported with evidence. If there are no internal sources of financial success, other sources exist. Satmetrix, the inventors of the Net Promoter Score® offer an e-booklet entitled *The ROI of NPS* (Satmetrix, 2017). In it they cite many examples of how customer experience has a strong payback based on:

- Higher retention rates.
- Increased upsell/cross sell opportunities.
- Lower cost to serve.
- Lower marketing costs due to word of mouth promotion.

We use Amazon as a role model for delivering great customer experience. Their commitment to great customer experience comes from Jeff Bezos, their CEO. Brad Stone, in his book, *The Everything Store* (Stone, 2013), tells how Jeff Bezos repeatedly pushed his staff to fill Amazon warehouses with all types of products with little or no financial justification that they would sell. In its formative years, as the company was growing, Bezos wanted to expand beyond books and movies, and offer toys. Predicting which toys and how many of them to have in stock prior to the Christmas season wasn't easy. What mattered to Bezos was that customers should have confidence in Amazon having the toy they wanted and that it would be delivered in time for Christmas. This fundamental component of customer experience has a high cost, for if the toy inventory is too short and product isn't available, customers will be dissatisfied. If the inventory is too high there will be toys left over which may not be saleable for another twelve months, if ever. This didn't deter Bezos who has an unswerving desire to satisfy the customer, without compromise and without consideration of the financial cost.

Those of you who feel that we are out of context quoting Amazon in a business to business book, beware. Amazon has its sights very firmly on B2B markets. Almost everyone we interviewed as a contributor to this book used Amazon as a pertinent example. Some felt threatened by it while others believed that they could supply a wider reach of customers through Amazon Marketplace. We certainly can learn a lot from it by observing its commitment to satisfying all its customers whether B2C or B2B.

Fulfilment

Only 38 per cent of B2B companies say they perform well on this factor (Cupman, 2016).

Fulfilment means understanding what customers want and meeting their needs. In Amazon's case it was making sure that the company had whatever products the customer wanted, that they could be ordered easily and they were delivered quickly. If this meant the company was overstocked with product and it cost millions of dollars in toys left on the warehouse shelves, so be it. The company had a promise to fulfil.

A brand is often defined as 'a promise delivered'. This means that a company should have a very clear proposition so customers know what to expect. It must then be set up to deliver against that proposition. Everyone in the company must be aware of the promise in order that they can ensure it is delivered.

Delivering excellent customer experience consistently to all customers, who may be very demanding, requires skill, patience and energy. It is not just the customer-facing team that has to be trained in customer experience. Fulfilment of customer experience may have to be carried out by people who are not aware that this is one of their responsibilities. For example, a production manager may think that their role in life is to produce products efficiently. While that may be an important part of their job, it shouldn't be at the expense of the customer. Long production runs for different product lines may be the best way of producing but it could mean some customers have to wait months before they can get the particular product they have ordered.

Fulfilment has a cost. The cost could be higher inventory, somebody's time or a change in behaviour. The realization that a new way of working means inconveniences or changes will be off-putting to some. Of course, new processes and ways of working can be imposed. An element of discipline and firm direction may be needed. But most of all, whoever fulfils the customer experience programme has to believe in it. If it is fulfilled under duress, the smiles will not be genuine, the heart won't be in it and the initiative will fail. This is why it is so important to recruit the right people into the fulfilment team. Once people see the success of the programme they will want to join. Nothing succeeds like success!

Seamlessness

Only 27 per cent of B2B companies say they perform well on this factor (Cupman, 2016).

Customers aren't interested in the internal processes companies use to run their operations. It isn't the customer's problem if a computer fails and the customer service desk can't access their details. They don't care if a company has procedures for health and safety that mean output is slower. This is not to say that customers are insensitive to health and safety issues or computer failures, rather it means they don't like these to be raised as reasons for poor customer service. They expect a company to be taking care of these on their behalf, ensuring minimal disruptions.

The way processes are joined up to deliver excellent customer experience is a supplier's responsibility. Successful restaurant chains are worth observing for the way they manage these processes. They often divide the job of looking after guests so that the greeting of the customer when they walk into the restaurant is by somebody in charge of booking, who knows which tables are available and when. A well-organized restaurant then seamlessly passes the customer to someone who takes the guests to their table. The waiter is now introduced as the person who will take the order and bring the food. If the restaurant is in the United States there may well be other service providers who top-up the water goblets and bring bread to the table.

The restaurant example is to illustrate that great customer experience doesn't have to be delivered by just one person. A business to business company can have someone take an order, someone deliver the order, someone answer technical questions and someone else deal with billing enquiries. Others behind the scenes may grease the wheels of the service delivery. As long as the team is joined up and knows what is expected of them, the service can be excellent and seamless.

In 2014 the Economist Intelligence Unit surveyed nearly 500 senior executives, the majority working for companies with annual sales of more than $500 million per annum (EIU, 2014). A complete range of industries were represented in the survey. More than a third of the executives (36 per cent) said that silos within their organizations were the biggest obstacle to providing better customer service. Around a quarter (24 per cent) said that a lack of senior management vision was the main problem for their customer service initiative. Three-quarters of the senior executives taking part in the survey said that a priority for their firms is to offer a better customer experience across all their different platforms. Whereas Amazon has just one platform from the customer's point of view (its website), B2B companies have telephone ordering via customer service desks, websites, emails and account executives calling in to take orders personally. These different platforms can have a big effect on customers' experience. Silos within organizations and the lack of integration between information systems can be a big obstacle facing business to business companies at the present time.

One of our contributors is a senior marketing executive in a global company and echoes the findings from the *Economist* survey:

'In a large company you can have people who are process driven. You don't make a decision unless a piece of paper tells you it's the right decision to make. We've got to have people in the organization that won't allow us to do anything that impacts adversely on what the customer gets. We need people who are intuitive about what is right when it comes to customer service. It puts more energy into the business.

The dilemma I have is "how do you go from medium to big where you have to put processes in and you don't get over processed so it impacts on the customer?".

I understand why you have to have processes but when does it start becoming detrimental to the customer and how do you pick up on this? When you add all these items together it makes you harder to deal with.

If customer service is really important to us as a company, should it be a central function and not isolated to a division?

We acquired a company recently and this company has a customer who spends about $1 million with us. He's got the same account manager and the same customer service executive as he had before the acquisition. Nothing has really changed for him. However, he has been talking about moving work away from us and he said we have changed. I asked him what was different for him. He said we have become bigger and it's not the same. He couldn't pin anything down because he was still getting everything he wanted and dealing with the same people. But he felt we'd grown too big and he felt it wasn't the same.

If I could make any changes it would be that every person in our business knew what customer experience meant to us from the top down. I want us all to be consistent around the touch points. I'd want our magic wand to let everybody know what customer experience means and we would train all the new staff to reinforce what it means. The second thing I would do is make ourselves easier to deal with and get rid of all the red tape so people have more autonomy to make decisions with the customer.

My advice to other people would be "don't let the processes take over." Think about the customer in any process that you do.'

Responsiveness

Only 40 per cent of B2B companies say they perform well on this factor (Cupman, 2016).

We have remarked in earlier chapters that speed of response is a critical component of excellent customer experience. A fast response lets a customer know that they are being attended to. The response should also set expectations. Thereafter, these expectations should be met and, if possible, exceeded. A customer's time is valuable as they have other things to do.

When the public is asked what the ideal customer experience is for them, they typically reply fast response to enquiries or complaints. They also look for simple purchasing processes. Business to business customers are no different. They look for fast responses though they are all too often disappointed.

B2B companies find it difficult to harmonize the different means by which they respond to customers. They have company websites with varying capabilities of transacting business and answering queries. It is quite normal when emailing someone in a B2B company to receive an 'out of office' reply informing that the recipient cannot be in communication for a day or two. Similarly, a direct call to the phone on an executive's desk is seldom answered any more. The call goes to voicemail before the executive decides whether they have time or the inclination to answer it.

Proactivity

Only 25 per cent of B2B companies say they perform well on this factor (Cupman, 2016).

Too often customers have to chase a supplier to find out what is happening to their order. The reason for the stony silence may be that the supplier is struggling to process the order. They may hope that as they delay any contact, somehow miraculously, the order will be fulfilled and they will be off the hook. It could even be worse if the supplier tells half-truths about the order, saying that it is being dealt with and raising expectations but creating a bigger problem to be solved later.

Customers like their suppliers to think ahead about what is needed. They want a supplier who will suggest different products that could better suit their needs. They want to know if there are better and more efficient ways to use the product and so lower the cost in use. They want products and services that give them an edge over their competitors.

Proactivity requires suppliers to fully understand the needs of customers to the point where they can second-guess what is wanted without being asked. There is no substitute for getting close to customers in every way. Visits to a customer's office and their factory could spark ideas. This happens every day with business to business sales representatives.

'We have an industrial gas salesman called Joe. Our reps visit customers to deal with problems and keep them happy. However, Joe spends a good deal of his time during visits ensuring that they have sufficient gas for their use. This is really important because if a customer runs out of gas it would bring their production to a halt. He looks for opportunities to install a telemetry device that automatically sends us an alert when the gas in the tank is low and then places an automatic order. When Joe does this the customer thinks he is wonderful because they are never under threat of being without gas. Joe is proactive in solving customers' problems and he has devoted and loyal customers.'

> 'Sean is a sales manager for a company that makes cardboard boxes. One day, walking through the factory of a large cereal manufacturer he could see the huge amount of space taken up by the store of cardboard packages for the filling lines. He suggested just-in-time deliveries, which freed up space that was subsequently used for a new filling line.'

Both Joe and Sean provided excellent customer experience by immersing themselves in their customers' businesses so that they could suggest solutions. They didn't wait for customers to ask, they were proactive.

Evolution

Only 39 per cent of B2B companies say they perform well on this factor (Cupman, 2016).

Customers are desperate for anything that will give them an edge over their competitors. If a supplier can think of ways to help the customer achieve their goals, it will gain customers' loyalty and a bigger share of wallet. New products, faster deliveries and cheaper processes will all be welcomed.

It is natural that customers want products and services that are better, cheaper, and faster. What may be new today will, in time, become the new norm. Customers get used to new ideas, competitors copy them and eventually they fail to provide an advantage. It is the same with the unexpected delights. Bowls of fruit at the reception desk of a hotel are no longer novel and hardly raise an appreciative eyebrow. Who wants another branded memory stick?

Customers' needs are changing all the time. Listening to customers and the front-line staff that supply them will help understand how these needs are changing. Customers can't always say what they want. They may not know what they need or what is possible. Consider the Sony Walkman. Akio Morita of Sony had the idea of a device that would allow listening to music on the move with a high fidelity set on the head. The general public had no idea that this was possible and would never have suggested it. People feed the ideas, the inventor develops the solution.

'Singapore Airlines has a difficult task on its hands (Wirtz and Johnson, 2003). It has built up a reputation for some of the best service in the business which means its customers have high expectations. Service has become an integral part of the Singapore Airlines culture but even so, the company recognizes the need to find ways of sustaining service excellence. They achieve this using their 40/30/30 rule. In order to achieve innovation for the customers they spend 40 per cent on training, 30 per cent on improving procedures, and 30 per cent on creating new products every year. They listen to feedback from all quarters. It is a holistic approach to service excellence. They are able to do this because customer experience is the central part of their culture.

This culture has resulted in them coming up with all sorts of customer experience innovations – book the cook service for business- and first-class customers allowing them to order their favourite meals before boarding, wide seats, Dolby sound and so on (Heracleous and Wirtz, 2010). However, it is the personalized service that makes the company special. The company's CRM system communicates birthdays, frequent flyers' names and favourite drinks to the cabin crew members. One of the authors of this book witnessed this commitment to a personalized service at first hand on a Singapore Airlines flight. He overheard a passenger ask if there were any car magazines on board. The steward disappeared and in less than five minutes was back with copies of Autocar and Car magazines. Where on earth he got them from goodness only knows. It was very impressive.'

Things to think about

- Do you have a plan for improving customer experience? Could you use PR Smith's SOSTAC® framework to drive the plan forward?
- How strong is the commitment to customer experience within your organization? What can you do to ensure unwavering commitment among the leadership team?
- How good is your organization at delivering consistent customer experience? Is this a training issue or a culture issue?

- To what extent is customer experience held back by silo mentality within your organization?

- What can you do to break down the silos?

- What sense of urgency exists within your organization when dealing with customers' requests?

- What can you do to improve responsiveness?

- How proactive are you with customers? How well do you understand their needs so that you can suggest better ways of solving them?

- How is your customer experience programme different today compared to last year or the year before? What can you do to keep it fresh?

- Which of the pillars will you major on in your customer experience programme?

References

Cupman, J (2016) The Six Pillars of B2B Customer Experience Excellence, *MarketingProfs*, 26 April [Online] available from: http://www.marketingprofs.com/articles/2016/29806/the-six-pillars-of-b2b-customer-experience-excellence [last accessed 16 February 2018]

EIU (2014) Creating a seamless customer experience – a report from the Economist Intelligence Unit [Online] available from: www.eiuperspectives.economist.com/ [last accessed 3 October 2017]

Heracleous, L and Wirtz, J (2010) The Globe: Singapore Airlines' balancing act, *Harvard Business Review*, July/August

Satmetrix (2017) *The ROI of NPS: How the focus on customer loyalty delivers financial gains* [Online] available from: http://info.satmetrix.com/ebook-roi-of-nps [last accessed 3 October 2017]

Smith, PR (2017) *SOSTAC®: The guide to your perfect digital marketing plan*, V3 [Online] available from: www.PRSmith.org/books [last accessed 3 October 2017] (SOSTAC® is a registered trademark of PR Smith. For more information on SOSTAC® Planning and becoming a SOSTAC® Certified Planner visit www.SOSTAC.org)

Stone, B (2013) *The Everything Store: Jeff Bezos and the age of Amazon*, Transworld Publishers, London

Wirtz, J and Johnson, R (2003) Singapore Airlines: What it takes to sustain service excellence – a senior management perspective, *Journal of Service Theory and Practice*, 13 (1), pp 10–19

Securing buy-in at all levels of customer experience 10

Buy-in at all levels

It would be wonderful if every customer experience programme was endorsed by someone at the top of an organization. We don't mean endorsed, we mean fully committed to at the head of an organization. Who wouldn't endorse the principle of customer experience? However, commitment is much stronger than endorsement. Commitment means that a real priority is given to the customer experience programme such that it will be favoured if choices have to be made between it and other business projects.

Commitment at the top of a company to a customer experience programme sends signals to everyone in the company about its importance. It is a key driver of a successful customer experience initiative. As we have seen in Chapter 4, only around a half of business to business companies believe that there is a true commitment to customer experience within their organizations. People may say that they are committed until times are hard, budgets get reviewed and the customer experience initiative is slashed. The reservations that hold back this commitment by the leadership team are usually concerned with money. If the leaders are convinced about the financial benefits of customer experience, they are likely to commit resource to the programme. In Chapter 3 we speculated that there are sceptics in business to business companies who would rather have a new machine or an extension to a warehouse than invest in another customer service rep.

Scattered throughout an organization there will be people who are passionate and committed to customer experience. By their very nature, people involved in sales are likely to be devotees of customer experience. This does not add up to a customer experience programme. A good salesperson can compensate for failures elsewhere within the organization. They can chivvy production and logistics to make sure that the product is delivered on time. They can placate the customer following an overenthusiastic letter from the credit control department. These are all vitally important responsibilities of a salesperson but they do not constitute a customer experience programme. A customer experience programme requires everyone within an organization to be devoted to delivering the highest levels of satisfaction to target customers.

Change at the coal face

Most people are enthusiastic about change. In fact, they can be very critical about things that don't change. They will say 'this company is like a fly caught in amber. It hasn't changed in years.' They will grumble that 'everything is the same, no improvements are ever made', that 'other companies are passing us by'. People know change is necessary. They know that without change a company will become a dinosaur.

Now ask individuals to change and they can feel very uncomfortable. Their routines that made for a comfortable life are under threat. They provide easy pathways to be followed day in and day out. The idea of change is one for other people, but not for me.

This is human nature and we should understand and respect it in our quest for a customer experience programme. Changes will be necessary in an effective customer experience programme and people have to believe the changes are worthwhile, otherwise the enforced change will be abandoned or delivered without warmth or conviction.

People will change if they believe that they will benefit and that there is something in it for them. Persuading people that there are benefits in approaching customers in a different way is not going to be easy if behaviours are ingrained. A strong incentive to change can be the example of others. John runs a wine club in Marple, and he told us the following story:

> 'I took early retirement from a senior manager's role in what used to be called HM Customs & Excise. We were the people who try to stop smuggling through airports and ports. I now run a wine club from my home. If you pick up the phone to place an order or if you email me, I will knock on your door within a couple of hours (or at any other time to suit you) with your wine. I like to make people happy and it isn't

that difficult. Everyone deserves smiles, a few pleasant stories, and a brief explanation for my high prices as they are signing the cheque. People have a choice. They can buy good wine from most supermarkets nowadays so there has to be a reason they buy from me. I have to give them that reason.

I have been asked how difficult it was to manage the transition from working for HM Customs & Excise to running my own small business. HM Customs & Excise is an authoritative public body responsible for dealing with people trying to import illegal booze and cigarettes. When I joined HM Customs & Excise many years ago, I had colleagues who were hard men. They didn't understand the concept of being nice. They didn't see how it was relevant to their job. They saw our job as cat and mouse – them and us. These people had a real problem when The Service started to refer to our targets as "customers".

I had a different view. Of course, I knew that we were dealing with people who were trying to break the law and hide things. However, I found that being civil, being fair, and often being nice, achieved great results. People were more likely to open up and confess. They were more likely to tell us what was going on. We achieved far more with my approach than the aggressive one.

Delivering a good customer experience isn't exclusive to an upmarket department store, it's something that we should all think about.'

Who would think that HM Customs & Excise is a believer in delivering great customer experience? It took people like John to set an example and show colleagues what could be achieved. John wasn't asked or forced to treat his 'customers' in this civil manner. It came naturally. John and his team didn't push their way of working down their colleagues' throats, they simply went about the job in a different way and over time their colleagues could see that John's way was better.

Dale Carnegie, in his book, *How to Win Friends and Influence People* (Carnegie, 1964), said 'Learning is an active process. We learn by doing.' He is making the point that adults learn best when they put things into practice, when they see things happening, and when they are convinced by results. When people see that something works and that it works better than the way they normally do it – and when they see that they could benefit – they are more likely to change their behaviour.

Change throughout the company

In business to business companies there may be a number of people in different positions who need to change how they work in order to improve the customer experience. Almost certainly sales representatives and customer service staff will need to change. The customer experience programme may indicate that some customers require more frequent calls than others, because they are big prospects. Re-adjusting the call frequency on the basis of customer size and opportunity may upset some sales representatives whose calling programme was based on companies they liked to visit.

Of equal importance will be changes that are required by other people within the organization. A production team that prefers to manufacture long runs of product in a planned sequence may need to show flexibility to accommodate a production run for a new or an important customer. A credit control department that has strict policies on credit limits may have to use its discretion and occasionally show a valued customer some leniency. Technical support teams may need to adopt a light touch every now and then when people complain about faulty materials or don't want to pay for advice. A customer experience programme requires commitment from everyone within an organization working towards the goal of satisfying customers.

Creating an internal service culture

Breaking down the silos within a company is critical. The silo mentality often exists because there is a lack of understanding of the bigger picture, especially within a large organization. People know that customers pay their salaries, but their first line of loyalty is to the department in which they work. This means creating an 'internal service culture' as most people within an organization only deal with internal customers.

A large logistics company described the problem they face breaking down the silos.

'We're trying to get everyone aligned to make it easy for customers to do business with us. Imagine that you go into a first-class hotel. The porter takes you to your room and tells you how everything works – where the gym is, the time breakfast is served, where there are local shops and amenities. It is establishing the customer's needs and nurturing them right

up front. That's exactly what we are trying to do with new customers. Of course we have silos but we are trying to show customers how they all fit together.'

Getting people within a company to see another department as a customer and serving them in the same way they would a paying customer requires a culture change. No money passes hands. No profit and loss account is dependent on the transactions between departments. Workshops involving different groups in the company provide an opportunity to explain the goals of a customer experience programme and the roles and responsibilities of different departments. Led by an experienced moderator, the workshop team can develop ideas for the change process and break down the barriers. Of course, this will be made all the easier if the activity of the group is openly supported by the leadership team.

Workshops and team briefings will help the mutual understanding between the departments but in all likelihood additional measures of performance will be required. Service levels between departments should be agreed and monitored.

Stop worrying about the 1 per cent of customers who take advantage

Businesses can be defensive about customers who complain that their products have failed. They may be justified. A customer may have bought the wrong product. They may have used the product in the wrong way. Consider for a minute what the implications would be if businesses adopted a generous returns policy similar to that of Nordstrom. For reference, Nordstrom's returns policy is extremely flexible. There is no time limit on returns or exchanges. There is no requirement that the product returned should have a receipt.[1] Nordstrom staff have the discretion to accept items of clothing that have been worn. Nordstrom believe that this generosity is worth it. Some customers may take unfair advantage but most repay the company with their loyalty.

The cost of a returns policy to a business to business company is likely to be significantly less than that of a retailer. Fashion retailers have high returns as people discover that the garment they have bought doesn't fit or the colour doesn't suit when tried on in the comfort of their home. A company buying a business product is unlikely to be fickle in this way. It is worth weighing up the cost of time and effort defending product claims versus adopting a Nordstrom view that the customer is always right.

Soften up the legal eagles

Businesses have become paranoid about litigation. Transactions that used to be settled with a handshake are now accompanied by lengthy service level agreements. Conversations between companies can only really get down to the nitty-gritty after signing nondisclosure documents. Emails are concluded with 100 unfriendly words threatening legal action if the note is forwarded to someone else. There are 67,000 corporate lawyers operating in the US alone (Domhoff, 2009).

With apologies to these lawyers, they are likely to see potential minefields with a generous customer experience programme. They are paid to look after businesses at the expense of third parties. They are not paid to be on the side of the customer. A company with a culture of great customer experience means having faith in customers. The vast majority of customers will be loyal and fair. We need to involve the legal eagles and get them to be supportive of the customer experience initiative.

Benchmark as much as possible

People are competitive. It is a great challenge to one department to know that another is performing better. Benchmarks can be a good way of encouraging change. Customer satisfaction scores and Net Promoter Scores® can be compared department to department or business unit to business unit. A department that is achieving high performance scores will prompt others to do better.

We referred earlier in this chapter to Dale Carnegie who was famous for his self-improvement advice. In his book, *How to Win Friends and Influence People,* he tells the story of how Charles Schwab, a steel magnate, used healthy competition and benchmarking to great advantage.

At the end of the day, just before the night shift began, Schwab asked how many heats the day shift had achieved. He was told that they made six. Schwab said nothing and just chalked a large number 6 on the floor.

When the night shift arrived they asked what the 6 meant. Word got around that the big boss had been in that day, asked how many heats were made. He was told it was 6 and he chalked the number on the floor.

The next morning the number 6 had been rubbed out and the number 7 was in its place. The day crew took up the challenge and left the number 10 on the floor when they had finished. The mill that had been performing badly in terms of production was now turning out more than any other mill in the plant. It was all due to benchmarking and competition.

When we carry out research into customer experience and we are presenting the findings, we cut the data to show the comparative results of different departments or business units. Where possible we show the results of companies in a competitive set. We know that the competitive itch recognized by Dale Carnegie will help to continuously raise the bar.

As we keep reminding ourselves, the comparisons are not just within a company or with competitors; increasingly our businesses are compared against the best in any class of quite different genres. These inter-company comparisons are entirely reasonable. If another company, albeit in a different line of business, can be innovative, easy to do business with and highly responsive, the business buyer asks why all companies can't be like that.

Table 10.1 gives an indication of Net Promoter Score® benchmarks amongst B2B companies. At the top of the league table are companies such as Apple and Amazon with Net Promoter Scores® of 60 or more. These organizations are B2C as well as B2B and they show what can be achieved among millions of customers. The average Net Promoter Score® for B2B companies is between 25 and 30. This is where we find many manufacturing companies. Service companies, including merchants and distributors, have made great efforts to build loyal customers and regularly achieve Net Promoter Scores® of between 30 and 50. Business to business companies with strong brands can enjoy similar scores and we discuss why this is so in Chapter 14.

Organizations with Net Promoter Scores® below average include oligopolies and monopolies. Their strong position in their markets hardens their attitudes to customers who are often exploited, ignored or treated badly.

Table 10.1 Typical Net Promoter Score® benchmarks for B2B companies

Net Promoter Score®	Performance	Type of company
Over 50	Excellent	Tech companies, boutique service companies
30 to 50	Good	Merchants, professional companies, strongly branded B2B companies
20 to 30	Average	Manufacturing companies, most B2B companies
10 to 20	Below average	Utilities, monopolies
0 to 10	Poor	Utilities, monopolies
−20 to 0	Very poor	Utilities, monopolies

There are a good number of reputable awards for customer service, including internal service. In the drive for improved performance, it could motivate a team to enter one of the award schemes. The purpose of the entry is to drive change in favour of improved customer service and the award is simply icing on the cake. If the participation in the scheme results in an improvement in customer service it must be seen as a great success and not a failure – award or no award.

Things to think about

- How committed is the leadership team of your company to customer experience?

- How siloed is your company? Which silos are the biggest barriers to improved customer experience?

- Where within your company is a good starting point for the internal service culture?

- What could make the leadership enthusiastic about an internal service culture?

- What initiatives could break down the barriers between silos and build a service culture between departments?

Note

1 Nordstrom's returns policy in their own words as stated on their website:
We handle returns on a case-by-case basis with the ultimate objective of making our customers happy. We stand behind our goods and services and want customers to be satisfied with them. We'll always do our best to take care of customers – our philosophy is to deal with them fairly and reasonably. We have long believed that when we treat our customers fairly, they in turn are fair with us. We do apply returns to the tender it was purchased with. If we choose to provide a refund and no record of sale is available, a return is provided at current price on a Nordstrom Gift Card.

References

Carnegie, D (1964) *How to Win Friends and Influence People*, Reed Consumer Books, London

Domhoff, GW (2009) *Who Rules America? Challenges to corporate and class dominance*, McGraw-Hill Higher Education, New York

Working with sales and marketing teams to streamline customer experience

The challenge of the large company

When customers contact a company it is for a purpose. Customers want quick and efficient customer service. They are not concerned who they speak to as long as the person can answer their question or deal with their problem. They don't care about titles, departments or company processes. They have their own agenda.

In a small company everyone knows the aims of the organization. People sit close together. They know what is going on everywhere in the company. As companies grow bigger and install more processes, there is a danger that customers' needs are forgotten. A large and dominant company may arrogantly believe that they know what is in the customer's interest – 'do it our way, or no way'. It is why commitment, fulfilment, seamlessness, responsiveness, proactivity and evolution are important pillars of customer experience. In Chapter 4 we saw that only 40 per cent of business to business companies believe that they are performing well in these respects.

Who owns customer experience?

In theory customer experience should be owned by everyone within an organization. This would be the ideal. It wouldn't matter who a customer speaks to within an organization, they would be delighted by the service they receive. Few organizations achieve this, especially business to business companies. People are recruited because they are technical experts, or geeks, or have expert knowledge that the company requires. They may or may not also have a disposition towards customer experience. Should these people be recruited if they haven't got this disposition? Of course they should. Business to business companies need experts in many fields and although it would be wonderful if everyone excelled at customer service, it is a wish too far.

If you want to judge the culture of a school, look at the headmaster/headmistress. Their influence is huge. So it is in most businesses. If the boss is a devotee of customer experience it will filter down to everyone including to the geeks, the introverts and loners.

However, there is only so much that the boss can do. They can set the tone and they can lead by example. They cannot be present at every touch point. In a large corporate organization, their influence will be diluted as their duties will be spread across a wide range of activities. In any case, there are multiple players within an organization that can make or break customer experience – customer services, sales reps, technical advice, credit control, marketing, product design, etc. Somebody needs to bring these groups together. If the boss has a true commitment to customer experience they will appoint a customer experience manager to champion the cause.

Department goals that are not aligned

Departments within companies have different goals. The sales department will have its own targets. These could be monthly or even weekly revenue and profit targets. The pressure to win sales and hit targets can override long-term plans of the marketing or customer service departments. In most business to business companies, sales teams are vitally important. People know that if the order book is lacking, profitability and ultimately their own jobs are at risk.

Sales teams in business to business companies do a great job. Salespeople are on the road performing the lonely task of winning customers and keeping them happy. It is a job that is performed individually, locally and not necessarily consistently across the company. Sales teams can be very precious about their customers. Salespeople who spend a good deal of time and effort winning their customers become fiercely protective of them and hate interference in this relationship by any of their colleagues.

Many B2B sales teams are focused on persuasion. They seek to persuade a potential customer to buy their company's products and do so by describing the many features and benefits. Most of this is redundant in today's world. Customers are capable of arriving at this analysis on their own; they know what they want and they can work out whether or not a company can supply it from websites and company reviews on the internet. Buyers today need salespeople who thoroughly understand their needs and can help their customers achieve their goals. The salesperson of today is a partner to the customer who can understand their needs and help the customer grow.

Marketing teams traditionally take the long view. They aren't focused on one or two or even 20 customers, as would be a salesperson. They are interested in all customers and potential customers who can be divided into groups depending on their needs and their opportunities. It is a generalization we know but sales teams tend to have short-term and local aims and marketing teams work to longer-term and broader vistas.

Marketing teams become frustrated if they feel that their efforts to generate leads are ignored by their sales colleagues. In turn, sales teams are vexed if they feel that marketers are sat on their backsides all day designing ivory tower schemes that don't work. Technical services are annoyed if they are called to solve a problem because a customer has been sold a product with a promise that was never possible. Customer service get exasperated if they work hard explaining to a customer that a product is in short supply while a sales rep, desperate to win the business, says it is available. It is easy to see how departments can sometimes pull against each other.

Aligning departments

Delivering consistent excellent customer experience is dependent on these silos working together. This is the role of the customer experience manager. Eight ways this can be encouraged are:

1 Find a big boss who takes responsibility for alignment

It is not unusual for a B2B company to have four or five departments spearheading sales and marketing. They could include field sales, customer service, marketing, promotion and product management. Some companies have separate customer experience departments. A company seeking to improve customer experience must bring together the disparate aims of these units.

In some companies this is achieved by appointing a vice president of sales and marketing whose job it is to make sure that the sales and marketing teams are aligned.

2 Involve the big bosses

Wherever possible get the teams together and have a senior person within the company address them on the subject of customer experience. The message should communicate how customer experience is critically important in the company's mission. The big boss needs to talk about the company's commitment to the six pillars in the customer experience strategy. The detail of the tactics can be left to the sales and marketing team.

3 Encourage communication

Communication is the answer to most problems. Sales and marketing teams don't always talk to each other enough. Daily communications would not be amiss. Has the sales team got the latest updates on customer activity? Are the sales leads working? What are the objections that are preventing sales? Are there any trends to take note of? Marketers also need to explain to sales what they do. Marketing needs to explain how sales leads are obtained and why they aren't perfect. They need to feed the sales teams with business trends so the salespeople can become business advisers and thought leaders to customers.

4 Develop personas

When Jeff Bezos of Amazon has a meeting, he leaves one chair empty. This is the customers' chair. Molson Coors does something similar. They bring into the room a life-size cardboard cut-out of the customer. Following customer research and its desire to improve its Net Promoter Score®, Molson Coors wanted the customer to be life-like so they developed life-size personas – one to represent 'promoters', one to represent 'passives', and one to represent 'detractors'. It is not unusual in meetings for someone to turn to one of the personas and say 'What do you think, Promoter Pat?' Having the customer in the room, if only metaphorically, keeps everyone customer orientated.

5 Design offices as community centres

At its Allentown headquarters, Air Products opened a coffee shop. The coffee shop is strategically located as a hub for people from all over the complex.

Just as commercial coffee shops make their environment a nice place to sit, drink and talk, so too Air Products provides an environment that encourages people to stay and mingle. A coffee shop of this kind or a nice restaurant environment can become an informal meeting place for people from different parts of the company.

Pixar uses the layout of its office to manage its culture. When the late Steve Jobs designed the Pixar headquarters he arranged the building around the central atrium so that staff would run into each other frequently (Egolf and Chester, 2013). The meeting rooms, the cafeteria, the coffee bar and the gift shop were all moved to the lobby area. In fact, the restrooms were moved to the lobby. He made sure that everything was set up so that people had to bump into each other.

6 Bring the teams into workshops

We know that we frequently mention workshops as a tool to achieve action. This is because they really do work. We are talking about workshops in which a mix of people from different departments can spend two or three hours working on a topic. In this way, people share their views and develop action plans, which means there is a good chance that things will happen.

Arriving at a solution may need a series of workshops, each one monitored to ensure that next steps are followed and the actions are implemented and followed through.

7 Focus on opinion leaders

In any group of people there will be someone whose views are respected. As a result, their advice and actions will be followed. Identifying these opinion leaders can weld departments together. Opinion leaders feed off respect and esteem and will respond to being brought in to the high-profile customer experience programme.

8 Encourage cross-team events

Being able to guarantee excellent customer experience requires everyone to understand the processes, their responsibilities, and be enthusiastic about its delivery. It is not just about cross-team training in workshops, it is also about the different teams wanting to help because they like and respect each other. Intercompany quizzes, finding their way out of escape rooms, or simply having time out together is important in fostering strong relationships between the teams.

Taking things for granted over time

Unfortunately, the idiosyncratic and different ways that customers are dealt with may not align with a company's brand, its mission or its objective to deliver customer experience. Sales teams can become lackadaisical. After the chase of winning an account and servicing it for many years, the sales team may take customers for granted. The dialogue with the customer settles into a regular chat about sporting fixtures rather than how the supplier can help the customer achieve its goals. The salesperson may fail to ask searching questions that uncover new opportunities believing that they already know everything there is to know about a customer.

Things to think about

- How closely does the marketing and sales team work together in your company?
- How can the marketing and sales team become more aligned to improve customer experience?
- What success has your company had in developing a needs-based segmentation? What are the criteria that would make this possible?

Reference

Egolf, D and Chester, S (2013) *Forming Storming Norming Performing: Successful communication in groups and teams*, iUniverse, Bloomington, IN

How to create an internal service culture 12

What is culture?

A small team of people or a department can begin the process of developing excellent customer experience. When this happens, the success will be coveted and the initiative should spread. Ultimately, the goal is for the whole company to embrace the culture of service orientation and the delivery of customer experience.

Culture is our starting point. A cult is a group of people with a very strong belief; often a religious belief. Members of a cult may be regarded as not quite mainstream – perhaps oddballs rejected by society. We need something of a cult for the service culture to really take hold. We need people who share a strong belief and passion in delivering great customer experience. These beliefs should be at the heart of a company's philosophy. This being the case, we would expect it to have a very strong influence on all management decisions and all business functions.

Our interest lies in the service culture as this is central to the delivery of an excellent customer experience. Service cultures differ between organizations. In the case of Amazon there is limited personal engagement between Amazon employees and customers. However, the company is passionate about keeping customers happy, almost fanatically so. In most business to business companies there is considerable personal engagement with customers and a strong service culture in the sales teams – but not necessarily in the rest of the organization.

Developing a service culture throughout a company requires employees to see that everyone they serve, work with and support, is a customer. The procurement team should see the production department as a customer because production needs the right product at the right time for it to function. The production team should see the logistics team as its customer because the logistics people need the product in the warehouses and on the trucks to fulfil promised deliveries. The accounts department looks after the payment of salaries, they pay vendors, and they manage the credit control of customers.

A company with a strong service culture has aligned all its employees with the value of a common behaviour – that of providing good service to everyone, internal or external.

The customer comes second

Rosenbluth International was formed more than 100 years ago in Philadelphia. The Rosenbluth family built the company into the world's third-largest travel management organization and it was bought by American Express in 2003. In the mid-1970s the company was turned over to brothers Hal and Lee Rosenbluth who recognized the opportunities in corporate travel. By 1998, 95 per cent of its $3.7 billion revenues were from corporate clients (Grant, 1996).

The success of the company was chronicled by Hal Rosenbluth in his book *The Customer Comes Second* (Rosenbluth and McFerrin Peters, 1992). The title is a tease because the fantastic experience they provided to their customers was the reason for their growth. The point made in the book is that this experience came from creating a special culture in which employees treated each other like clients. The service and professionalism that began in the office then spread outward to customers.

Great care was taken to find the right people to join the company. They looked beyond the skills of their potential recruits and sought out people with the right attitude. In particular they avoided arrogant people, egotists and opportunists. Above all, they looked for 'nice people who care' in the belief that everything else could be taught. This follows almost to the letter the principles taught by Heskett in *The Service Profit Chain* (Heskett et al, 1997).

Support from the top

A service culture cannot be imposed with a flick of a switch. It requires a sustained and consistent effort over a long period. There are many factors that are necessary for the service culture to develop and grow.

We have constantly referred to the importance of senior management support for a customer experience culture to flourish. A management dictate will not work; it requires a genuine commitment to providing customer service. One of the many impressive stories told about Jack Welch, the leader of GE for 20 years until 2001, was that he was difficult to get hold of during the spring and fall of each year as he spent a good deal of these hours with major customers (Welch and Welch, 2015). Although GE was a complex organization with strong beliefs about production and finances, under Welch, keeping the customer happy and understanding their needs was paramount. He led by example.

Hiring the right people

We cannot emphasize enough the importance of recruiting people who are eager to serve. Look for the tell-tale signals at the recruitment interview. Does the candidate smile often and easily? Have they ever served in a restaurant? Have they ever worked in a phone unit? Have they ever conducted charitable work? Spend time making sure you get the right people. It is an expensive process for sure but it is far less expensive than constantly hiring, training and firing.

Jim Collins, in his book, *Good to Great* (Collins, 2001), argued that one of the most important requirements of a successful company is getting the right people on the bus and then getting them in the right seats. Recruiting the right people is the starting point. This is very much the case with developing a strong service culture.

In conversation with Chris Daffy, a customer experience guru (Daffy, 2011), we asked him the $64,000 question, 'what makes a great customer service person?' He didn't hesitate.

> *'I used to think you could train anyone in customer service. Certainly training makes a big difference. However, if you want people to deliver good customer service, you have to hire people with the right attitude. Some people just love serving others while others find it difficult. You will always have problems with a service culture if there are people who just don't get it.'*

This was what Jim Collins was getting at when he says 'They start by getting the right people on the bus, the wrong people off the bus, and the right people in the right seats' (Collins, 2001). This takes us back to the importance of the need for people in the organization to believe in the culture for it to be effective.

Hal Rosenbluth has a good deal to say on hiring the right people (Rosenbluth and McFerrin Peters, 1992). He makes the point that in their selection process they look for kindness, caring, compassion and unselfishness rather than an impressive salary history and lots of degrees. He says:

> 'You can't teach people to be nice. You can't just say, "Thursday, begin caring!" Caring must be inherent in their natures – they have to feel it in their hearts. And if they do, their clients will feel it too.'

The people who contributed to this book repeatedly emphasized the importance of employing the right people and inculcating them with the right culture.

> 'If I had a magic wand the thing I would change would be people. I want people who have empathy, people who will listen, people who will care, people who will help customers and people who believe in what we're doing. I want people who want to achieve the success that we are going for. It is about building culture. We need to explain the culture and get everybody aligned. We need to make sure the customer is high on the agenda. Our managers shouldn't just be talking to their staff about skills, they should be asking about their interactions with the customer.'

Training

Once you have the right clay, you will be able to mould it to shape. Training is essential as it is important to achieve consistency in the way that customer experience is delivered. The clay needs to be moulded in the same way every time. Employees must understand how the service culture is vital to a company's goals, mission and vision. Training ensures alignment. It is a continuous process.

Constant training is what keeps Singapore Airlines as an exemplar of delivering excellent customer experience (Wirtz, 2003). The company regards this as a necessity for everyone from office assistant to baggage handler and chief executive officer. Everyone is sent for training regularly. This includes training on functional skills and also on the softer skills.

Everyone in Singapore Airlines is trained in the company's core values. In this way the philosophy of customer experience is shared throughout the organization. As might be expected, it is the cabin crew who are the critical touch point between the company and passengers. Their basic training programme lasts for months. As well as the functional skills it covers softer skills such as communication between people of different cultures, personal poise and dealing with demanding passengers. In order to qualify for this training, the cabin crew will have gone through a rigorous three-stage interview that weeds out candidates whose personal values do not align with those of the company (Chong, 2007).

Cabin crew members learn how to greet passengers, the importance of making eye contact with everyone they meet and, of course, the importance of the smile.

Training doesn't stop after the four-month immersion process. It involves role-playing that gets pilots to act as ground staff, ground staff to act as engineers, engineers to act as cabin crew and cabin crew to act as pilots. Everyone learns the art of service and the common language of how it is delivered – not just to customers but also to colleagues.

Empower people

We have all suffered from the 'jobsworth'. You phone a company with a problem and are passed from pillar to post. No one will accept responsibility for your problem. In their words, 'it's more than my job's worth'.

Customer-facing people are often low in the hierarchy of any organization chart. They are lowly paid and there is likely to be a high churn as they move between jobs. Their commitment to the company where they work is often fragile. If this is true for front-line staff, it would be difficult to trust them to use their own judgement when dealing with customers' problems.

Companies that take more trouble to recruit the right people, train them and give them guidance in delivering excellent customer experience will not feel the same way. Nordstrom, who we have cited already, allow their employees the power to serve customers as best they can. They do not have a bureaucratic returns policy which means that employees can use their discretion to provide the customer with the best service possible.

Communication

The experience that is delivered to a customer may follow a complex chain. Addressing a customer by their name as they sit in an airline business-class seat requires the booking details to have been accurately recorded in the system and placed into the hands of the cabin crew. If the computer suffers a glitch or the customer decides to swap seats, it is very easy to make a mistake with this simple task. Communication is at the heart of this process. The right data must enter the system and the system must be capable of producing the right data and the instructions at the point where they are needed. The communication has to get to the right person and it isn't easy. One of our contributors emphasized the importance of systemizing communications with customer service staff by making sure they get the right emails at the right time.

> 'One of the things you've got to get right is how you get consistency and how you communicate it across the whole organization. We have three people at the centre who control the communications throughout the whole organization. They manage the daily, weekly and monthly communications that go through to the front line. It stops the front line getting the millions of emails they used to get. They now get them in a controlled way. They get emails each week that tell them how the week should be structured, what they should be doing on certain days. Then there's a monthly comms that keeps them up to speed with the latest communications. We try to make the message that goes to the front line consistent. The challenge is delivering on the consistency. Telling people what we are doing and what to do is easy. Ensuring that they are consistent is the tricky bit.'

Rewards and awards

The delivery of excellent customer experience should be recognized. At its very simplest, management should thank the teams that deliver customer experience. A thank you costs nothing and goes a long way.

There are more formal means of recognizing service excellence. Many companies have schemes that nominate an employee of the month or an award that could be accompanied by a certificate and a prize. Rather than reward individuals it may be more appropriate to encourage effective teamwork with an emphasis on all the members that helped achieve the success. The awards can be within a company or in competition with others across a nation such as the UK Customer Experience Awards, which is entered by 200 different companies.

Increasingly bonuses are linked to customer experience. Measurements of customer satisfaction and the Net Promoter Score® are frequently used as a component in bonus payments. This is not always without issues as the measurement process has to be robust, otherwise people can feel that they have been unfairly treated and the scheme backfires.

Things to think about

- Culture trumps strategy. What is your company culture and is it suited to delivering excellent customer experience? How consistent is it throughout your company?

- To what extent is your HR policy geared to customer service? Are you recruiting the right kind of people to provide excellent customer experience?

- What training do people receive on delivering excellent customer experience? How far does this training extend throughout your organization?

- How good are your communication systems in providing people with the data that is necessary to deliver excellent customer experience?

- Do you have incentives in place that reward excellent customer experience? What incentives could work in your organization?

References

Chong, M (2007) The role of internal communication and training in infusing corporate values and delivering brand promise: Singapore Airlines' experience, *Corporate Reputation Review*, **10** (3), pp 201–12

Collins, J (2001) *Good to Great*, Random House, London

Daffy, C (2011) *Once a Customer, Always a Customer: How to deliver customer service that creates customers for life*, Oak Tree Press, Cork, Ireland

Grant, T (1996) *International Directory of Company Histories*, Vol 14, St James Press, London

Heskett, JL, Sasser, E and Schlesinger LA (1997) *The Service Profit Chain: How leading companies link profit and growth to loyalty, satisfaction, and value*, The Free Press, New York

Rosenbluth, HF and McFerrin Peters, D (1992) *The Customer Comes Second*, William Morrow & Co, New York

Welch, J and Welch, S (2015) *The Real-Life MBA: Your no-BS guide to winning the game, building a team, and growing your career*, Harper Business, New York

Wirtz, J and Johnston, R (2003) Singapore Airlines: What it takes to sustain service excellence – a senior management perspective, *Journal of Service Theory and Practice*, **13** (1), pp 10–19

Using segmentation to deliver better customer experience

13

People and companies are not all the same

Companies are not all the same, nor are the people that work within them. This is a very obvious point. However, many companies treat their customers as if they are the same. For sure we tend to react a bit quicker and jump a bit higher for larger customers. But how many of us group our customers according to those who want a close partnership, those who want innovation, those who want lots of services, those who want a low price and nothing else? Business to business companies are not very good at recognizing their customers' different needs. And yet, the recognition of customers' needs is at the heart of marketing. The whole philosophy of marketing is based on meeting different customer needs to ensure their full satisfaction.

Most business to business organizations segment their customers according to their size and their industry vertical. This makes a lot of sense. Big companies present big opportunities because they buy lots of products. It is not unreasonable therefore that they receive lots of attention. Companies in different industry verticals may buy different products. Sales teams find it easy to recognize companies of different sizes and in different industry verticals. They only need look up the company in a directory or drive up to its offices to find out what type of company it is and where it fits into a simple segmentation based on size or industry vertical.

The problem with a segmentation based on size and industry vertical is that it takes no account of customers' needs. It is like firing a storm of arrows at a single target. Each of the arrows is an offer from the company. Some will find their mark and others will hit the target but not the bullseye.

A survey of customers' needs is likely to show that there are some customers that want lots of one thing and not another. Some may want service, others a stripped-down transactional offer. Yet others could have more specific needs. An examination of the types of companies within these different groups of companies would most probably include a cross-section of companies of different sizes and in different verticals. Four common needs-based segmentations in business to business markets are shown in Figure 13.1. Here we are showing them according to the main factor that drives their choice. They may end up with completely different labels. For example, the price-focused segment may be given a title such as 'transactors', 'price seekers', 'penny pinchers', etc.

Now imagine that each of these groups of companies representing different needs is a target. Arrows will be selected for each target and will therefore have a much greater chance of hitting one of the bullseyes (Figure 13.2).

Segmentation and customer experience

In our experience as business to business market researchers we estimate that within any group of customers, around a fifth to a third are very price conscious. Of course, they also want products that perform. However, they don't demand the services that are often associated with business to business offerings. They want straightforward transactions that deliver value for money. They are price fighters.

At the other end of the spectrum are companies that want a good deal of support from their suppliers. They want technical advice, frequent communications, special deliveries and so on. They value these 'add-ons' and are prepared to pay for them.

Sat in the middle are companies that may be migrating from a transactional position into one requiring more support.

A company that treats all customers the same will inevitably fail to satisfy some. In fact, some companies may not be organized to deal with certain types of customers and shouldn't chase them. Recognizing that some customers are not suited to your offer can be hard for a sales-orientated company that is eager to sell to anybody and everybody. A blunderbuss approach to marketing is sure to deliver lower levels of customer satisfaction brought down by these misplaced customers. Equally, targeting certain customer types that you know are more suited to your offer will deliver high levels of satisfaction through the improved customer experience.

Figure 13.1 Common business to business needs-based segments

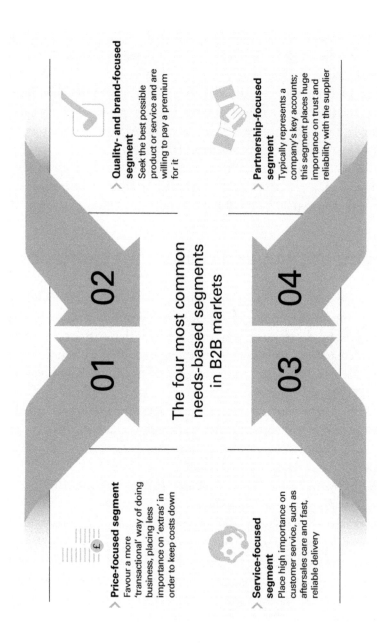

The four most common needs-based segments in B2B markets

01

> **Price-focused segment**
Favour a more 'transactional' way of doing business, placing less importance on 'extras' in order to keep costs down

02

> **Quality- and brand-focused segment**
Seek the best possible product or service and are willing to pay a premium for it

03

> **Service-focused segment**
Place high importance on customer service, such as aftersales care and fast, reliable delivery

04

> **Partnership-focused segment**
Typically represents a company's key accounts; this segment places huge importance on trust and reliability with the supplier

SOURCE Used with permission from B2B International

Figure 13.2 Hitting targets by breaking markets into segments

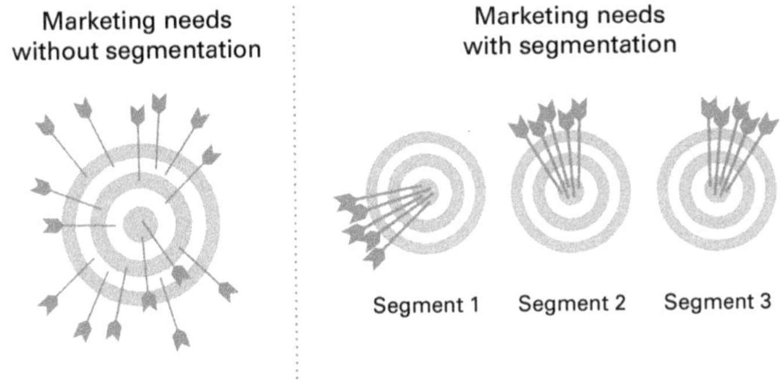

Marketing needs without segmentation

Marketing needs with segmentation

Segment 1   Segment 2   Segment 3

Dealing with the decision-making unit

Segmenting business customers is more demanding than segmenting the general public. The decision-making unit in businesses is more complicated. Whereas in a household there will be a limited number of people choosing the furniture or the foodstuffs, in a business there could be a range of people involved in the decision. The business to business decision-making team could involve board members, production managers, health and safety people, a procurement team and technical experts.

This complication in the decision-making team can often be resolved by examining the customer journey (see Chapter 8). At certain points in the customer journey different people will be involved. A technical person may have a higher involvement early on in the decision-making process when the specification of a product is being approved. Procurement people get involved when price negotiations are taking place to choose between two or three suppliers. Logistics people become interested once supplies are under way. There are usually one or two key decision makers and these are the people who are central to the segmentation. Working out who has an influence at different parts of the customer journey will help direct the right messages to the right people just when they need it.

The test of a good segmentation is the degree to which customers' needs really are different. We are looking for clear blue water that separates one group of customers from another. Only in this way can customers and potential customers be allocated to specific segments. When customers are safely in their segments they can be accorded the products and services they want – and will be happier as a result.

Segmentation and product proliferation

Recognizing customers' different needs can lead to a problem of product proliferation. Before we turn our mind to B2B markets, let's for a minute close our eyes and walk down the aisles of a large grocery store. We are in the section that sells toothpaste. How many different types of toothpaste are on the shelves? A visit to www.colgate.com shows that the company has 47 different toothpaste products. Search for toothpaste on Amazon and it will list over 4,000 products although admittedly that includes dog toothpaste. In the grocery store there will be toothpaste featuring fluoride. Some toothpastes are designed to minimize plaque and some control tartar. There is toothpaste for sensitive teeth and toothpaste that will make your teeth whiter than white. There is special toothpaste for smokers. They come in tubes of different sizes, pump packs and bottles. Do we really need this much choice? The explosion in products is the result of eager product managers who feel they have to make their mark and fill a niche with something new.

It is the same with industrial products. A customer might ask for their product to be modified and a new version is happily added to the company's product portfolio. Over the years the product list of a B2B company gets extended and eventually could run to hundreds of variations. All have been relevant at some time to someone. Many clutter the product portfolio and could be axed at no loss to customers. In fact, a more focused product line may make it easier to locate what is required and improve the customer experience. What makes it worse is that many of these different products are given brand names. Not only do we have product proliferation, we have brand proliferation.

Henkel has become a global market leader in industrial adhesives. Over time it acquired and built up a large portfolio of hundreds of product names and brands, which became too complex for many customers to navigate. A good number of the so-called brands weren't brands at all but codes by which the product could be ordered. It found that many of the old brands could be simplified and consolidated under the Henkel and Loctite names. The new approach, which concentrates on only a few brands, has more impact and reduces the confusion among customers and potential customers (Henkel, 2017).

We have to face up to the fact that customers demand different versions of products and customer experience is enhanced by meeting these various needs. The skill is in segmenting customers into manageable groups so that they have products that meet their needs and that make economic sense to the supplier. Some obvious product segmentation possibilities are:

- Companies that like a wide choice of products versus companies that opt for a narrow choice.
- Companies that like products that are bundled as part of a package versus companies that like to pick and choose what they are buying and from whom.
- Companies that like to buy products supported by lots of technical service versus those that want products with no service.
- Companies that like innovative products versus companies that prefer products that have been tried and tested by others.
- Companies that like products with a strong brand name versus those that are unconcerned about the brand name.
- Companies that judge the value of products on their cost in use versus companies that buy simply on price.
- Companies that stay loyal to a product versus companies that like to switch and try products from new suppliers.

We are sure there are many more product segmentation possibilities. It is worthwhile thinking about how your customers can be segmented in terms of their product requirements. Once a segmentation of this kind is in place it will be possible to better serve their needs with the right customer experience. Segmentation is hard to get right – it should always be under review, as one of our correspondents says:

'We used to assume all our customers were the same whether they had one delivery a year or one delivery a day. Now with our larger customers we have dedicated resource for them. However, they still all come through the same call centre. Everybody is dealt with exactly the same. We are still struggling as to how we should deal with the different sizes of companies that come through the call centre. What does one hotel owner experience against someone from a hotel chain? What is the persona of those different interactions? What is it that drives them and what are their needs? We get it on the domestic side where we have 30,000 customers but not on the B2B side where we have a 3,000 customer base. Does a small hotelier or a pub or a restaurant have similar needs? We haven't got to that yet.'

Arriving at a business to business segmentation

We have talked about the importance of segmentation and the benefits of delivering better customer experience by recognizing customers' different needs. We should now turn our attention to how to arrive at an appropriate segmentation.

In Darwinian fashion, it is likely that the companies you currently do business with have a good fit with their needs and your offer. Extending the segmentation into the wider market and including potential customers would be an added complication. Start with a segmentation of your customers and not the whole market.

We will assume that you have a comprehensive and up-to-date list of customers you can work with. The aim will be to populate this list with as much intelligence as possible. Some things will be obvious and easy to obtain such as the customer's address, the name and title of the contact, the products they have purchased, the frequency of purchases, the quantities, etc. This data needs converting into numeric codes so they can be analysed. The addresses could be coded with a number to identify their location in the North, South, East or West – or coded by state or county; whatever is relevant. The titles of the contacts could be given a numeric code according to whether the respondent is in procurement, production, technical, administrative, etc. It may be thought appropriate at this stage to code the gender of respondents and possibly their age. You never know, a demographic characteristic may show up different attitudes and needs; millennials do sometimes act and think differently to baby boomers.

The volume of business carried out with customers should be coded in some fashion such as small, medium or large. At this early stage we recommend removing the very largest customers – the ones that are key accounts and critical to the business. Such is their importance, these 'big dogs' need to be treated individually. The segmentation process will now be applied to the remaining companies.

Most information in the customer database will be factual firmographic data. What you need in order to have more insights on each customer is additional intelligence that tells you something about their behaviour, attitudes and needs. Some insights on customers are easier to obtain than others:

- Easy – behavioural data showing the number of years the company has been a customer.

- Easy – behavioural data showing the range of products and services that the customer buys.

- More difficult – behavioural data showing the proportion of business placed with your company versus that given to competitors.

- More difficult – attitudinal data that people have to suppliers, environmental pressures, etc.

- More difficult – needs-based data indicating the importance attached to value for money, credit terms, quality of products/services, delivery options, visits and service from salespeople, innovation, etc.

Obtaining data on attitudes and needs is not as straightforward as it may seem. It is here that needs-based segmentations get into difficulties. Of course, there is no problem asking somebody why they chose a company as a supplier or what their attitude is to environmental factors and the like. However, they will usually offer a rational and trite explanation such as 'we look for the best price, and we want great quality and fast delivery.' We have already discussed the influence of emotional factors on the buying decision and we know that it is difficult for customers to concede their importance. Furthermore, what is important today may not be important tomorrow. If products are in short supply right now this may be the number one factor influencing the choice of supplier. When the supply situation eases, its importance will most likely be taken by something else. And how do we take account of the fact that the 'decision-making unit' is made up of buyers, technical people and production people, all with different needs?

Difficult though it may be, it is worth coding and classifying customers using as much data as possible. When customers are grouped and clustered together there may be some obvious segments that stand out. Some companies may be diehard price-driven. Some companies may always be eager for a wide range of products and services. Recognizing these key groupings of customers will start to show the possibilities for a needs-based segmentation. There nearly always is a group of companies that are transitional between a couple of polarized segments and want a bit of everything.

When a segment begins to take shape it should include a group of customers with a strong disposition towards a particular offer. This means that a separate marketing plan will be required for each segment. It makes sense therefore not to have too many segments as each will incur a marketing cost in supporting its special requirements.

Arriving at a segmentation that is best for you

The segments that emerge should pass what we called the 3D test. Each segment should be measured in terms of it being:

- Distinctive – if there aren't any distinctive attributes to the segment, it will be hard to recognize and introduce new customers to it. Marginal differences in needs are not enough to justify a different segment.

- Desirable – each segment must have a strong need for the products and services you offer. If a segment doesn't have a resounding appetite for what you are selling, it isn't a segment you will want to serve.

- Durable – segments need to stand the test of time. Companies are put into segments and expected to stay in them for a year or two. If you place a company in a segment that has changing needs, your marking plan will be out of date before you know it and the messages you use to target companies will create dissonance.

A segment that fails on any of these three factors should be reconsidered and possibly set aside as one that is not for you or collapsed into one of the others.

Coding different attributes of companies in an Excel spreadsheet will allow you to sort and group companies to see what segmentation possibilities exist. It will be easy to recognize different firmographic segments such as companies of different sizes or in different geographical regions. However, because it is easy do this, it gives you no competitive advantage. Your competitors will most likely be doing the same. It is the segmentation possibilities based on behaviours and needs that are more difficult to derive and copy and have the potential for giving you a strong competitive advantage, especially in delivering high levels of customer satisfaction and experience.

When we search for groups of people with different needs, there will not be one single factor that is important; there will be a bundle of factors that drive choice. In our search for these combinations of factors we need help from statistics and we turn to factor and cluster analysis. Factor analysis focuses on the attitude attributes and reduces them to a small number of component factors; groupings of attitudes that can be empirically linked. Cluster analysis focuses on the respondents themselves, putting them into relatively homogeneous groups on the basis of their attitudes to what is on offer. One cluster may prefer products that are simple, straightforward and low-priced and may be characterized by a label such as 'transactors', indicating that they want very little except the product itself. Another cluster may be made up of companies of different sizes and in different industry verticals, all wanting a partnership and prepared to pay for it. They may be labelled 'solution seekers' (or something similar) in order that everybody can quickly and readily understand their key characteristic. More detail on the mechanics of developing segments in business to business markets can be found in another Kogan Page book by the authors (Hague *et al*, 2016).

Problems with needs-based segmentations

Hopefully this discussion on segmentation will have indicated that statistics or a simple sorting of data in a spreadsheet can suggest different groupings. The choice of segmentation has to be that of the company that is going to use it. Firmographic segmentations are possibly the most popular in business to business markets because they are easy to recognize and easy to implement. Furthermore there is a good logic to forming groups of big, medium and small customers so that they can be given the appropriate attention and resource.

Behavioural segmentations are great because the way companies behave is a good clue as to their needs. How companies act and behave is very visible and makes for a segmentation that is easy to implement.

Needs-based segmentations are hard to achieve but they are the Holy Grail as it is through understanding customers' needs and addressing them that customer experience can be improved (see Figure 13.3).

Needs-based segmentations are not without their problems. Whereas it is easy for a sales rep to place a customer in a segment according to its size and its vertical market, it is much more difficult to locate a customer in a needs-based segment. In theory the sales rep can ask what the customer is looking for and identify needs through simple questions. However, a shrewd customer may be inclined to tell a salesperson that they are looking for a very attractive price if only because they know that this is their opportunity to strike a good deal. In fact, the same company may be interested in lifetime costs, high levels of service and be prepared to pay a premium, though they won't admit this to a sales rep or a researcher.

Figure 13.3 The road to a needs-based segmentation

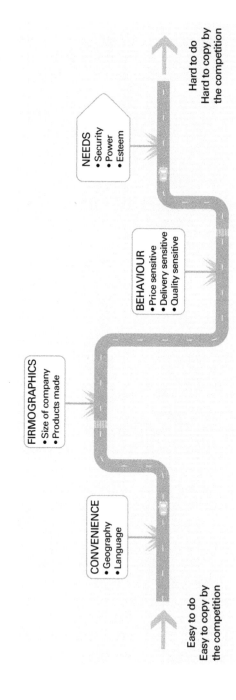

CONVENIENCE
- Geography
- Language

FIRMOGRAPHICS
- Size of company
- Products made

BEHAVIOUR
- Price sensitive
- Delivery sensitive
- Quality sensitive

NEEDS
- Security
- Power
- Esteem

Easy to do
Easy to copy by
the competition

Hard to do
Hard to copy by
the competition

SOURCE Used with permission from B2B International

Profiling the segments

Once the segmentation has been agreed, a detailed profile should be created to show key characteristics. These could include the following:

- The most important factors that drive the selection of a supplier.
- Important firmographic characteristics that may help identify companies within the segments, such as their size and industry vertical.
- The importance of different decision makers within the segment and any variability in their needs.
- The numbers of companies in the segment, the revenue and profit generated by these companies.
- Named examples of companies that typify those within the segment.

Beyond the easily recognizable characteristics of company size and industry vertical, there may be other factors that influence customers' needs. These are the attitudes of the people that work in the company and their culture. These are psychographic drivers. Some companies are always looking for new suppliers and regularly switch from one to another. Other companies demonstrate long-term commitment to their suppliers, indicating high levels of loyalty. The behaviour of companies can be a good indication of needs.

Making the segmentation workable for the salesforce

A well-meaning marketing team could devise a segmentation of customers that is unworkable by the sales team and create a rift between the departments. Marketers can be blind to the practicalities of implementing a needs-based segmentation. In most business to business companies, sales teams trump marketing teams because the former bring in the revenue. This means that if a sales team wants to kill a proposed segmentation they can do so. Working together, the marketers and the sales team can arrive at a segmentation that gets closer to meeting needs and so improves customer experience. And crucially, they must arrive at a segmentation that is implementable.

A supplier of aviation fuel to airports carried out a survey of its customers across Europe. Data from the survey suggested that there were four segments with quite different needs. One group of airports looked for high-quality fuels and ease of ordering. Another placed a premium on being able to quickly rearrange their orders in response to changing requirements. A third segment placed an emphasis on customer service and a fourth one was very price driven. The fuel supplier adopted a needs-based segmentation and it proved a huge success, as told by the marketing director of the company:

> 'When I came into this job as marketing director we saw airports only in terms of their size. Everyone found this a simple and easy way of looking at our customers. However, when we looked at our satisfaction ratings we saw that they were much lower with our biggest customers. We needed to do something different. We decided to group our customers according to their different needs. What made the new segmentation successful for us was the change in attitude of the salesforce. The salesforce no longer visited customers saying "how are we doing today supplying you with fuel, can we sell you any more?" On every visit they asked questions designed to find out what the customer really needed, how we were performing against those needs, which companies were doing a better job than us, and what we would have to do in order to make the customer more satisfied. Our reps liked it because their visits were more stimulating and they found out so much more about their customers. Customers liked it because they could see we were interested in understanding them better and solving their needs. Two years on we have adjusted the segments slightly as our depth of understanding of customers has increased. The result has been a dramatic increase in our satisfaction scores and an improvement in sales revenues and profits.'

General Data Protection Regulation (GDPR) – applicable to the European Union

Segmentation requires us to use data on companies and individuals and this means we need to be aware of data protection legislation. In May 2018 new European Union regulations apply and anyone wanting to sell to people or companies within the EU will have to abide by them. These regulations are known as the General Data Protection Regulation or GDPR.

There are a number of things to bear in mind when considering GDPR:

- The regulation is designed to protect individuals. This is an important point for business to business marketers. There is no problem maintaining information on companies. A database that lists companies and the amount of products they buy, the frequency with which they buy them, and the attitudes and needs of that company can be kept legitimately in a database for purposes of analysis. However, data kept on individuals within those customer companies is bound by the legislation. This does not mean to say that you can't keep an email address or classify a customer according to whether they are a millennial or a baby boomer, but it does mean that you have to have an appropriate legal basis for doing so. For customers of private companies, this includes the necessity of processing data for the performance of a contract or some other legitimate interest. In other instances, consent may be required from individuals and it is worth obtaining it when they sign up as a customer with some words such as the following:

We may use the information you provide to us to better understand your interests so we can try to predict what other products, services and information you might be most interested in. This enables us to tailor our communications to make them more relevant and interesting for you. If you don't want us to do this you may opt-out here

Note that there has to be an opt-out clause that, if checked, would mean you cannot keep profiling data on this individual. We predict that most customers will not opt out as they will understand that the data is held for legitimate purposes to try to ensure that their needs are fully met.

- Someone has to be responsible for taking charge of the data and using them correctly. This someone is the organization that collects and processes the data and is known as the 'data controller'. Companies cannot do things without people and so within your company you will need a named individual (or individuals) who have the responsibility for this task. You will also need a 'privacy policy' that is clearly signposted on your website and other company literature.

- Should a customer ask to see what information is held on them, you are honour-bound to share it with them. The customer could object to your use of this information for direct marketing or profiling purposes, in which case it would be necessary to remove this personal data from your database.

An excellent guide to GDPR can be found on www.bluesheep.com (Blanchard and Smith, 2016).

Things to think about

- How up-to-date is your customer database? How comprehensive are the details you have on your customers?

- How do you segment your customers at the present? What do you consider the strengths and weaknesses of this segmentation? How does it help you deliver a better experience to your customers?

- What are the possibilities of segmenting your customers based on their behaviour or needs?

- What additional data do you need from your customers to be able to carry out this analysis?

- In what way do you think behavioural or needs-based segmentation will help you serve your customers better?

- What barriers, if any, are there in your company that could prevent you introducing a needs-based segmentation?

- How readily will your company's sales team accept a needs-based segmentation and what will induce them to do so?

- Do you do business with any companies in the European Union and, if so, are you organized to meet the needs of the General Data Protection Regulation?

References

Blanchard, S and Smith, R (2016) The General Data Protection Regulation (GDPR) – A practical guide for businesses, Blue Sheep [Online] available from: http://www.bluesheep.com [last accessed 20 November 2017]

Hague, P, Cupman, J, Harrison, M and Truman, O (2016) *Market Research in Practice*, 3rd edn, Kogan Page, London

Henkel (2013) Henkel Adhesive Technologies New Branding, 2012–2014 [Online] available from: http://henkeladhesivesna.com/iframes/ae_brands/AE_2012-2014_Branding_Customer_Presentation_Sept_2013.pdf [last accessed 15 November 2017]

PART FOUR
Implementation of a customer experience programme

The role of brands in creating better customer experience

14

The role of the brand

There is a general supposition that decision making by business to business buyers and specifiers is entirely rational. Business to business buyers are seldom likely to admit that they choose a supplier because 'they like them'. When has an engineer ever said that he or she specifies a supplier because 'they make me feel important'? It is far more likely they will say that their choice is driven by the quality of the product, the price, the speed of delivery and so on. And yet, many companies have suppliers that have been in place for years and years. Surely there must be something else going on that is driving the buying decisions?

So what is going on? Maybe we are wrong in believing that the buying decision is largely rational. We know that emotions play an important part in consumer markets and we know that people don't leave emotions at home when they go to work. How much of the buying decision is influenced by emotions? It is hard to say but some people argue that it accounts for up to half of the decision – even in traditional business to business markets (Newman, 2014).

If we assume for the moment that emotions do play a role in influencing the buying decision, perhaps a larger role than we have previously admitted, then we must find some means of measuring this. The brand of a company is where we are likely to find most of the emotional repository because brands create an expectation and expectations carry with them a great deal of hope and promise. This is the stuff of emotions.

When we buy a product or service it nearly always has some means by which we can identify it. There is the name of the manufacturer or supplier, there is a logo and very often we have a pool of knowledge on the company. All this adds up to a perception of the product and the company. This perception translates into an expectation. If our knowledge of the company or product is scant, our expectation will be limited. If we know a good deal about the company, we will have a high level of expectation. This expectation is the promise made by the company. It is its brand. There is an old saying that 'a brand is a promise delivered'.

The name and the logo of the company are important recognition symbols. Upon recognition we think of all the values, good and bad, attached to the brand. These values are often referred to as equity as they are an asset of the brand. Creating a strong brand builds the equity in a number of ways:

- It draws people to the product – a brand that is well-known quite clearly has a better chance of being selected than one that is not known.

- It gives people a reason to buy – the promise of certain values makes a product distinct and draws people to it.

- It generates loyalty – a brand that successfully delivers against its promise creates trust, which allows people to buy in confidence time after time because they know what they will get.

Brands light up emotions

Emotions are the feelings we have about a brand. The emotions can be negative, in which case they destroy the value of the brand, or they can be positive and build equity in the brand. Colin Shaw has written widely on the subject of customer experience and how emotions drive value. He identifies emotions that destroy brand loyalty (Shaw, 2007). He lists these as:

- irritated;
- hurried;
- neglected;
- unhappy;
- unsatisfied;
- stressed;
- disappointed;
- frustrated.

The main positive emotions he says are:

- trusting;
- focused;
- valued;
- safe;
- cared for.

He sees some other emotions as those that grab attention in the brand:

- interesting;
- exploratory;
- energetic;
- indulgent;
- stimulated.

The list is not exhaustive and there may well be specific emotions relevant to different brands. Once the emotions attached to a brand are identified, the degree of association of the emotion with a brand and its competitors can produce a sort of DNA. Some brands will be more associated with emotions than others and to that extent will have different DNAs. Understanding the emotions of a brand and that of a competitor's is important in the strategy of improving customer experience. Experiences and emotions are fundamentally linked. If we know which emotions are owned by our brand, we can foster them so that the customer experience is heightened.

The association that a brand has with certain words and images can be used to establish where it is strong and weak. This is what Colin Shaw calls an 'emotional signature'. Just as our own signatures are unique, so too emotional signatures are distinct and can be compared with those of other companies.

Using brands to differentiate

Many business to business products and services are seen to be very similar. They are made to specifications and in many cases are regarded as commodities. That said, they are not commodities as the 'offer' is never exactly the same even if the product is to a matching specification. Each company will have different ways in which orders can be placed. It will have different delivery schedules, different attitudes to dealing with problems, different terms of payment, different people will speak to the customer, etc. These service attributes are just as much a part of the offer as the physical product and they make it distinctive.

The components of an offer, many of them service promises of one kind or another, constitute the brand promise. A brand is an important means by which differentiation is achieved. We know this to be the case in consumer markets. Although people will claim to be experts in the taste of cola drinks, in blind taste tests most people struggle. In studies where people are asked to taste Coca-Cola and Pepsi, brain scans have determined that the enjoyment of the drinks is much increased by knowing which brand is which (McClure *et al*, 2004). It is why Coca-Cola and Pepsi-Cola are able to achieve significant premiums over 'own brands' and local brands. It is the same with wine. If we know the brand (and the price) of the wine we are drinking, there is a good chance it will influence our experience when we taste it.

People who make decisions in business are the same people who drink cola and wine. They have perceptions like anyone else and they can be influenced. For example, a 25 kg bag of black bitumen macadam for repairing potholes in the road can vary in price by more than 300 per cent. The product in each case is black asphalt with a polymer that allows it to be laid cold. The brand is a key differentiating factor. The more expensive varieties have dedicated websites, advice on laying the asphalt and imply a strong technical strength to justify their price premium. It is their marketing that differentiates them.

Adding value

Differentiation gives people a reason to buy and gives a company an opportunity to charge more. Exploiting perceptions by charging more may seem like a sleight of marketing hand. It isn't. People get pleasure out of wearing branded clothes, they like driving certain makes of cars, they seek to eat at restaurants with 'a big name'. If the pleasure is more because the brand is strong, then value has been created. Much of life is a mind game and so conditioning the mind to appreciate products is perfectly legitimate. Marketing is also expensive and the cost of building the brand must be recouped somehow from its price.

Business to business branding

With some exceptions, a lot of business to business companies have neglected their brands. It is as if business to business companies feel that branding is only for consumer products. Their belief in the excellence of their product and their relationship with their customers may be all that they think matters. However, their relationship with their customers *is* their brand. The problem is that this relationship isn't always nurtured as a brand. Maybe the company doesn't care about how its website looks as long as it is technically brilliant. Maybe no one worries if each sales representative promotes the company in a different way as long as they achieve their sales targets. Maybe there is no vision for the brand of the company and therefore there is no attempt to align everything within the company towards that vision.

There are a number of things that business to business companies should think about to develop their brands and so improve customers' experiences.

Have very clear values for the company

Values define a company. They indicate what its actions are likely to be when under pressure. They need to be true values and not over hyped. If they are true values, they will be beacons for everyone within the company and, when necessary, defended to the hilt.

Vision and mission statements can get out of hand but they have their purpose. Values are a kind of essence. Values are what are left if everything in a company is distilled to just one or two things. Too often companies develop mission statements that are long and complicated and no one can remember them. The brand essence is captured by just one or two words or a simple phrase that describes the heart of the company. Here we are not talking about the objective of the company being to make money. This is a by-product of why a company exists. Nor are we talking about the products a company makes. What we are looking for is the reason for a company's existence. It is what Simon Sinek calls 'start with why' (Sinek, 2011).

Sinek asks questions such as 'Why is Apple so innovative? Why do they have something different when they have access to all the same things as the competition? Why were the Wright brothers able to achieve powered flight when there were others with more resources capable of doing it?' He explains the reason for the success of great companies and great leaders with what he calls the golden circle. 'Why?' is in the centre of the circle, 'how?' forms the next concentric ring from the centre and 'what?' is the final concentric ring on the outer part of the circle. (For 'why?' think 'Why does my company exist?'; for 'how?' think 'How does my company do business?'; for 'what?' think 'What does my company offer?')

Sinek argues that every organization knows what they do. Some know how they do it but very few know why they do what they do. The inspired organizations all communicate from the inside out – from the why to the what. For example, Apple seems to say to us 'everything we do challenges the status quo, we believe in doing things differently, we challenge the status quo by making our products beautiful to look at and they work really well – do you want to buy one?'

The limbic system, which sits right in the centre of our brain, is the bit that is responsible for feelings and trust. It is the limbic brain that is responsible for human behaviour and decision making. When we communicate from the inside out we are communicating directly to the limbic system. We can give people all the facts and figures about a product but they still do something different because to them it doesn't feel right. A company that is successful believes in itself and so its employees will work harder for it because they too believe in it. Customers will stay loyal because they also believe in it. As Sinek says, 'people don't buy what you do; they buy why you do it.' The 'why' is the essence of the brand.

Align staff with the company values

When the values of your company are agreed, everything within the company should be aligned to meet them.

For many years Domino's Pizza made '30-minute delivery' a core guiding principle. This became so strong a claim it guaranteed to meet the 30-minute claim or the customer could have their money back (Hart, 1988). Eventually the 30-minute guarantee had to be stopped as the company suffered lawsuits from accidents caused as some of its agents were so bought into the offer that they drove dangerously in an attempt to deliver on time (Janofsky, 1993).

Virgin Atlantic has as its mission 'To embrace the human spirit and let it fly.' There is a clear aim here to release emotions in customers and staff. It is resonant with freedom and getting away from things. It is a great promise for an airline that whisks people to new experiences and destinations.

Quickbooks' mission statement is slightly longer but it makes sense – 'To improve our customers' financial lives so profoundly, they couldn't imagine going back to the old way.' That is clear. It tells us that Quickbooks is out to make a big difference to financial livelihood and everything they do will point in that direction.

ADM is a business to business company that processes oilseeds, corn and similar products and develops feed ingredients for livestock. Its mission statement is 'To unlock the potential of nature to improve the quality of life.' Short, snappy and indicating the importance of their products in improving our lives.

Microsoft's values are 'To help people and businesses throughout the world realize their full potential.'

In all likelihood everyone within these companies will know the mission statement and what it means. They will understand that everything the company does should be delivered against these brand values. If a company can align its staff against the 'why?' it will get the belief that Simon Sinek says is so important because people don't buy what you do; they buy why you do it.

Consistency in everything the company does

A good brand should always deliver against its promise. If the promise doesn't change, the delivery of the promise shouldn't change. The brand should be consistent.

The devil is in the detail with branding. In needs to be so if consistency is to be achieved. The way the brand is portrayed is usually subject to strict guidelines. These guidelines will instruct how the logo is used, how much white space is allowed around it, the exact colours to be used and so on. This is just the logo.

In addition there should be consistency in other details that signify the company. The way the phone is answered, the way that emails and letter-heads are laid out and signed, and the formatting of presentation documents should all be to a formula so that they are clearly recognizable as coming from that particular company. It used to be possible to recognize IBM employees by their dark blue suits, white button-down shirts, rep ties and wing-tipped shoes. Although the conformity of dress may be more relaxed nowadays, other aspects of branding within companies are strictly adhered to. This consistency of the brand gives customers the reassurance that the next time they buy from the company they will get what they have always received in the past.

Things to think about

- What influence do you believe your brand has on the decision to choose your company as a supplier?

- What are the values of your brand that have most influence on the experiences enjoyed by your customers?

- In what respect is your brand distinct and different from competitors' brands?

- What is the 'why' of your brand? Do customers and potential customers know the reason for your company's existence?

- To what extent are you building and developing your brand to deliver an enhanced customer experience?

- To what extent are all the people in your company aligned with the values of your brand?

- How consistent is the delivery of your brand? What inconsistencies need to be brought into line to strengthen the brand?

References

Hart, CW (1988) The power of unconditional service guarantees, *Harvard Business Review,* July/August

Janofsky, M (1993) Domino's Ends Fast-Pizza Pledge After Big Award to Crash Victim, *The New York Times*, 22 December

McClure, SM, Li, J, Tomlin, D, Cypert, KS, Montague, LM and Montague, PR (2004) Neural correlates of behavioral preference for culturally familiar drinks, *Neuron*, **44** (2), pp 379–87

Newman, D (2014) How Personal Emotions Fuel B2B Purchases, *Forbes* [Online] available from: www.forbes.com/sites/danielnewman/2014/05/07/how-personal-emotions-fuel-b2b-purchases/#31b77a3053b0 [last accessed 31 October 2017]

Shaw, C (2007) *The DNA of Customer Experience: How emotions drive value,* Palgrave Macmillan, Basingstoke

Sinek, S (2011) *Start With Why: How great leaders inspire everyone to take action,* Portfolio Penguin, London

The role of products in creating better customer experience

15

Product – the heart of the offer

We are constantly referring to the importance of service and relationships in creating excellent customer experience. You may be wondering if we have dismissed the importance of 'the product' itself. Most certainly not. The product is at the heart of any offer. It is what people set out to buy to satisfy their needs. A great product provides a wonderful customer experience that lasts a long time. To us 'product' means everything people receive when they buy something, including any supporting services. If that product is wrong for any reason, the memory of it lasts even longer!

One of the reasons Apple achieves high customer experience scores is the excellence of its products. When you receive an iPhone it is in a box that is so impressive people often keep it, simply because it seems too good to throw away. The phone itself delivers beyond expectations. Little things about it delight people. When an iPhone user found out that you can delete an entry made on the calculator by swiping the screen left or right he posted his discovery on YouTube and within a couple of weeks it became a hit view. People expect the phone to work and it does. Things such as the calculator with its neat features that impress are a bonus that adds to the delight. It is another reminder, if we need one, that customer experience is at its strongest when it is unexpected.

Selecting the product

People begin to experience a product before they make a purchase. There is nearly always a period of exploration early in the customer journey. A very large percentage of B2B buyers say that they conduct some form of online research before purchasing a business product (Accenture, 2014). People are hungry for information on a new supplier or product. If they have never bought from the company before, they almost certainly will seek information online. A company's website is an obvious place to seek information at this early stage and it could have a big effect on the decision. The appearance of the website, the ease of navigation and the access to specification data can be highly influential.

Blogs and reviews are taken seriously. If the product is available on Amazon (and many B2B products are), people will take as much interest in the reviews as they do in the product photo, the specification and the price.

Online sources are not the only means by which people collect information on companies and products. If the product is sold through distribution, a visit to a merchant could provide an opportunity to examine the product itself. If the product is complicated or of a high value, the prospective customer may ask for a reference visit – an opportunity to see the product working in a real environment. The prospect that has got this far is showing real interest in the product. If it performs well and the reference is positive, there is every chance that a sale will be made.

The audience for acquiring knowledge could range from a designer or technical person through to a procurement specialist wanting to find a best offer. In consumer markets most of this searching is carried out on mobile phones in and around the marketplace. In business to business markets much of the searching is done on personal computers though mobiles are quickly gaining ground. Speed is essential in optimizing this experience. People will quickly move on if a site takes too long to load or they can't immediately find what they want (Google, 2015).

Product packaging

The packaging of products is of obvious importance in consumer markets. Packaging protects products during transport, promotes products from the shelves, and it carries instructions and information that will be useful to the person that buys it. The role of packaging is no different in B2B markets but it is surprising how its potential can be neglected. Trucks that carry the product provide a moving platform for communicating with a wide audience and yet it is not uncommon for this free billboard to feature a company name and nothing else. It is a wasted opportunity to build customer experience.

The packaging used for industrial and B2B products is often utilitarian. Sacks and boxes of products are despatched with very little information. The large blank spaces on the packs are unexploited opportunities to provide application advice or at the very least some words that reinforce the decision to purchase.

A walk around a customer's warehouse may show that the customer has scrawled on the packs or pinned notes to them. These are obvious clues to a supplier as to how the labelling of the packs could be improved. A supplier of office paper products placed jokes inside its packs in an attempt to give its products personality and to make the brand more human.

The packaging provides important protection, but once this role is fulfilled it may be an encumbrance to the customer. Cardboard boxes need to be flattened and recycled. Business buyers, like the general public, are concerned about sustainability and excess packaging can rankle. Wooden pallets must be stacked and take up space before they are removed. Empty cans must be removed safely and at minimal cost. A supplier that understands these problems and takes care of them for the customer may be providing a much-valued service that wins customer devotion. Increasingly B2B customers don't just buy products, they buy solutions.

The audience exposed to the packaging may be different to that which enquired about the product during the exploratory stage. It could include warehouse people, logistics staff, operational and production workers. Procurement and technical people who had an earlier interest in the product and who placed the order may not have any involvement in this later stage. The people who deal with the packaging may not be key decision makers in the sense that the choice of supplier has already been made. However, their role increases in importance as regular deliveries are received. They are able to endorse the choice of supplier or be critical of it to the point where they can exert pressure on the key decision makers for a change.

Product use

We are talking about business to business products as if they are all the same and, of course, they are not. A useful way of classifying B2B products is according to whether they are strategically important to the purchaser and whether the expenditure on the products is high or low. Customer experience will play a different role depending on the type of offer.

In the south-west quadrant of Figure 15.1 are products on which a company spends very little relative to other things it buys. They also are of

Figure 15.1 Strategic importance of products vs spend matrix

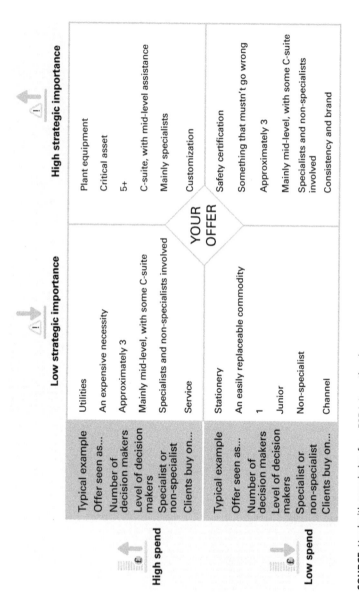

	Low strategic importance	High strategic importance
High spend		
Typical example	Utilities	Plant equipment
Offer seen as...	An expensive necessity	Critical asset
Number of decision makers	Approximately 3	5+
Level of decision makers	Mainly mid-level, with some C-suite	C-suite, with mid-level assistance
Specialist or non-specialist	Specialists and non-specialists involved	Mainly specialists
Clients buy on...	Service	Customization
Low spend		
Typical example	Stationery	Safety certification
Offer seen as...	An easily replaceable commodity	Something that mustn't go wrong
Number of decision makers	1	Approximately 3
Level of decision makers	Junior	Mainly mid-level, with some C-suite
Specialist or non-specialist	Non-specialist	Specialists and non-specialists involved
Clients buy on...	Channel	Consistency and brand

YOUR OFFER

SOURCE Used with permission from B2B International

low strategic importance. Typical of these are stationery products such as paperclips and writing pads. Because of the small expenditure and the low strategic importance of the products, the decision to choose a supplier is usually vested in one person. This does not mean these products are of no consequence. They are important components in every company's day-to-day operations. A manufacturer of two-ring binders or flipcharts can find plenty of opportunities for delivering excellent customer experience. Buyers are impressed by innovative products and outstanding service. There is also the opportunity to build strong brands that give comfort to the purchaser who may be quite unsure whose products to select.

In the north-west corner of the matrix are products where there is a high expenditure but which are of low strategic importance to the buyer. Utilities (electricity, gas, water, etc) or the raw materials used in factories are illustrative of products in this quadrant. Opportunities for improving the customer experience may lie in the way the products are delivered, offering flexibility around delivery times, improving product packaging and focusing on elements of service that would differentiate the commodity status of the products.

Moving now to the north-east corner we meet products that are purchased because they are strategically important and which incur a large spend. The plant and equipment used in a factory exemplify products in this quadrant. These products are almost certainly heavily branded and multifunctional teams of three or more people are often involved in the purchasing decision. Each person in the decision-making unit may look for something different and so there are many opportunities for delivering excellent customer experience.

Finally, in the south-east corner are products that are strategically important but where there is only a modest expenditure by a company. This is the province of services such as safety certification, accountancy services, legal services and market research. The group of people who choose suppliers for these products or services will be middle or senior within an organization. Again, there are many opportunities for offering excellent customer experience to these decision makers.

Improving customer experience by product design

Wherever a product sits in the matrix, there are opportunities to improve the customer experience. Product features are easy to compare. We see this all the time on comparison sites. It is also very easy to compare prices.

Usually products are compared within a price band. As might be expected, the most significant features and benefits will be compared. And yet, what may appear quite a trivial aspect of a product may be something that elicits a high score on customer experience. We return yet again to the adage that little things matter when it comes to customer experience.

We may not even know what is pleasing to us about a product. When you look at an iPhone you may get pleasure from its appearance without quite realizing why. Walter Isaacson in his biography of Steve Jobs tells the story of how Jobs was obsessed with rounded corners (Isaacson, 2011). He thought that sharp corners just didn't look right. The story goes that Jobs had lengthy discussions with Bill Atkinson, the Apple engineer who developed software that would accommodate his rectangles with rounded corners. Atkinson broached the difficulties of the design but Jobs got his way and no doubt he was right. The Lisa computer, later the Macintosh and finally the iPhone are all design icons. We look at these products and they just feel right. The rounded corners are one small element of the design that improves the customer experience even though it may be subliminal.

A company buying a product has expectations of its performance. Customers anticipate that the products they buy will work in a certain way and that they are made to specified and consistent quality standards so when put to use they will work as imagined. There will be expectations of reliability, durability and performance. All of these expectations are variables with some users accepting a higher level of tolerance in quality standards than others.

It is at this point, during the use of the product, that its true value can be recognized. A raw material that is more expensive than alternatives may be easier to process and so have a lower cost of manufacturing. A cheaper product may fail more often and result in increased warranty claims for the company, so raising its cost in use. Unless a company takes these efficiency calculations into consideration, the buyer may not know its true cost to the company. Understanding how products are used and their cost in use will help a business to business company position its products competitively. This information can be obtained from conversations with customers' operational staff or by carrying out ethnographic studies in which observers watch and record what happens in a customer's production environment.

The augmented product

We are using the term 'product' loosely. To some people the product refers simply to the physical item that is purchased. To others it includes much

Figure 15.2 The augmented product

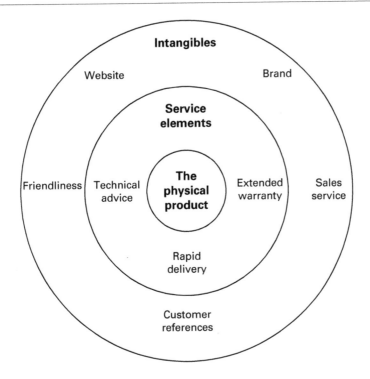

more – it is the total offer. This could include the warranty, service backup, rapid delivery and even some softer features such as a strong brand. This extended offering beyond the physical product is often referred to as the augmented product (see Figure 15.2).

It is around the augmented product, especially those elements beyond the physical product, that there are many opportunities for improving the customer experience and achieving differentiation. One of our contributors told us how they had augmented their product.

'Our product is no different to anybody else's. It is made to an industry specification so it has to be the same. Everybody's deliveries are the same – they have to be. This means that the only thing we can compete on is the price. At least that's how it used to be. It was the rocky road to ruin. Everyone competed on price, our margins were constantly being squeezed. We employed a company to carry out ethnographic *research. The researchers placed people in our customers' production departments where they watched what was going on, took photos and talked to people on the shop floor. We thought we had the perfect product. It was delivered on strong wooden pallets. We didn't realize that these wooden pallets were a real pain for the customer. They were piled up inside and outside their factories. No one wanted them as they weren't a standard size and it cost a lot of money to dump them. We looked around and found someone who could supply us with pallets made out of cardboard. They are quite strong enough and can easily be disposed of in recycle bins. That single change was welcomed across all our customers. No one else has copied us yet but no doubt they will in the future and then we will need to think of something else.'*

The changes that make a difference seem obvious once they are explained. It is why researching customers' needs is so important. When we asked one of our contributors what advice they would give to B2B marketers trying to achieve differentiation they said:

'The advice I would give someone is to get insights. When I started the job I didn't value insight as much as I do now. You need to get into the detail of what the customer needs and have analytics that you can drill into to get an understanding. We thought we were really good and when we explored our customers in depth we found there were things we need to do that we hadn't realized. We have been poles apart in the past. You can be going the wrong way before you know what you've done. And, it's not just the insights, it's how they are delivered. You need to get your CEO and operations manager to understand these insights because they don't see this sort of information every day. We've got to get them to buy into it straight away. We've got to get our senior team to buy into it because if they don't, change won't happen. It's not just insights, it's how you display them and how you use them.'

Things to think about

- Where do your company's products fit in the matrix of strategic importance versus spend?
- What are the characteristics of the decision-making unit and their product needs?

- What is it about the physical aspects of your product that people like? To what extent are these physical aspects unique?
- How strong is your augmented product? What makes it strong?
- How do the service aspects and intangibles of your offer make your product more appealing?
- How can you segment your customers in terms of their product needs? How could you use this segmentation to improve customer experience?

References

Accenture (2014) 2014 State of B2B Procurement Study, Accenture Interactive [Online] available from: https://www.accenture.com/t20150624T211502__w__/us-en/_acnmedia/Accenture/Conversion-Assets/DotCom/Documents/Global/PDF/Industries_15/Accenture-B2B-Procurement-Study.pdf [last accessed 3 October 2017]

Google (2015) *Micro-Moments: Your Guide to Winning the Shift to Mobile*, Google [Online] available from: https://think.storage.googleapis.com/images/micromoments-guide-to-winning-shift-to-mobile-download.pdf [last accessed 3 October 2017]

Isaacson, W (2011) *Steve Jobs*, Simon & Schuster, New York

Price and its role in creating better customer experience 16

Price expectations

We have talked a lot about customer experience being based on expectations. Nothing sets expectations like prices. The price of a product automatically positions it in our minds. If it has a high price tag it is reasonable to assume that the product will come with lots of benefits. A lower price tag infers fewer benefits. Almost every market has a choice of good, better and best products and they will have associated prices. If we were to plot these products on a graph where the two axes are price and benefits, we can expect (theoretically) to see the products distributed along a line that splits the axes at 45 degrees. This is the value equivalence line (VEL). If a company or brand sits to the left of the line it could be expected to lose market share; its perceived price isn't commensurate with the benefits of its offer. A company positioned to the right-hand side of the value equivalence line would be expected to gain market share. Over time, most brands gravitate towards the line. In the car market Volkswagen Audi group own a number of brands and, diagrammatically, they would be distributed as in Figure 16.1.

Price, the value buster

There is an old saying, 'you remember the quality long after you have forgotten the price.' If the product is worth it, you are happy to pay the price. The problem is that many customer experiences are destroyed by prices.

In B2B and B2C markets suppliers sometimes try to confuse us with complicated pricing packages. This may result in a temporary boost to

Figure 16.1   The value equivalence line for Volkswagen Audi brands (schematically)

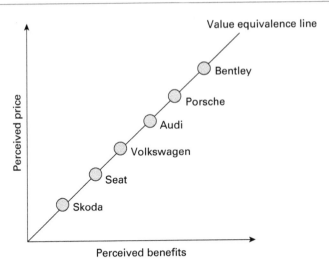

profits but in the long run it creates dissonance. It doesn't take customers long to get wise to the fact they are paying over the odds for a product and when this happens, they feel ripped off. Nor is it possible to bamboozle them for long with extra charges for packaging, certification or delivery, which weren't mentioned at the time of placing the order. Many industrial gas buyers are not happy about the rental charges they have to pay on gas cylinders. Customers buying ready-mix concrete get annoyed when they have to pay extra to pick up the concrete themselves. Some customers have to pay an additional phone charge when they ring in to place an order. Banks are capable of slipping in unexpected fees when you're not looking. Mobile phone companies offer businesses plans that are unnecessarily complicated. Lack of transparency in pricing creates mistrust, especially when the outcome is a price that is higher than anticipated. These are pricing tricks that disrupters love. It provides fertile ground so they can enter the market with simpler pricing that enables them to quickly build trust and market share.

Trends in B2B pricing

Things are changing, at least in some areas. There are still attempts to confuse customers on prices but, in the main, prices have become simpler and more transparent. Your journey with Uber involves no cash although, of course, a price is transacted. You pay, tip included, directly to Uber and you know the price of the journey in advance. You know where you are up to. This convenient and simple pricing mechanism is considered a better experience than a traditional taxi ride where sometimes you are lucky if the driver will take a credit card.

When you buy from Amazon you can see the price of your products. If your bank card details are logged with the company, one click will allow you to make a purchase. Call in at Starbucks and you can order your coffee and cake, and pay with a contactless card. It isn't like the old days where you totted up the cost of your purchased items, exchanged notes and counted your change. Price hasn't taken a back seat but it has become a more seamless transaction.

This is the situation in consumer markets. The business to business buyer is missing out on many of these changes. Business to business companies are often less than transparent with their prices. This obfuscation used to be a source of profit. Electrical contractors buying cable received huge discounts and the list price meant nothing. Each contractor thought they were doing really well with their massive reductions until in conversation with another contractor they would find out someone else's discount was even more. Discounts still exist in many business to business markets and are dependent on negotiations. This lack of candour and attempts to negotiate the best price has delayed or stopped many business to business companies from posting their prices on their websites.

It is not surprising that business to business buyers want the same seamless transactions they enjoy when they buy consumer products. The gap between consumer and business to business purchasing is disappearing. B2B companies are no longer isolated. The business to business buyer sees what is possible when they buy consumer products and it raises the very obvious question, 'why can't everyone be like that?'

The cosy, comfortable world of B2B pricing is coming to an end. Disrupters are everywhere. These companies choose markets that are deliberately complicated and where customers are ripped off by convoluted price structures. Tesla has cut out the car dealer and sells its cars in retail malls off a price list. Amazon is bringing its simple purchasing platform to B2B buyers with Amazon Business. Skype is becoming a mainstream competitor in business to business markets with Skype for Business. Car dealers, maintenance and repair suppliers and telecoms companies need to watch out.

Becoming more customer centric using price

In the drive to customer centricity it helps if the CEO is on board. The CEO will be on board if convinced that any changes to the pricing model will improve the bottom line. At its simplest there are just three ways to improve profitability – sell more, charge more or reduce costs. We will deal with each in turn and see how it relates to customer experience.

Reducing costs

A company can take cost out of its business model and in doing so it can increase profitability. If it splits some of these savings with customers and lowers its prices, it can use its price advantage to win market share and improve profitability. This is the way of many disruptors. Selling direct to customers allows them to remove distributors who historically have taken a 25 per cent margin to stock and distribute the product. Dealing direct with customers has an additional cost but by saving the distributors' margin there is a lot of saved cost to contribute to reduced prices.

Incumbent suppliers don't find it easy to remove the distributors. The large incumbent suppliers lack experience in dealing with a myriad of small to medium customers. They are slow and inflexible with their fee-paying public. Distributors provide the customer interface and deliver the customer service and experience. Without distributors the large companies are vulnerable; with distributors they are expensive.

Disrupters haven't yet hit business to business markets with the ferocity of their impact on consumer fields – but they will come and the place to start is services. DocuSign is disrupting the sleepy legal world with its electronic cloud-based e-signature technology. SurveyMonkey is disrupting the market research industry with its free or low-cost DIY questionnaires and analysis software. Ezetap is an Indian disrupter that is seeking to make payments easy, from large enterprises through to thousands of small retail businesses, using digital technology (CNBC, 2017).

Almost without exception disrupters are newcomers in a market. It needs a newcomer to make a dramatic change because incumbents won't give up their goose that is laying the golden eggs. It is why Kodak went to the wall even though it was the company that invented the digital camera in 1975 (McAlone, 2015). Launching the digital camera would have threatened the company's profitable film sales.

Disrupters make their mark by stealing customers who buy from traditional suppliers as well as selling to new customers who have never bought these products before. This is possible if you are selling low-cost taxi rides or phones that double as cameras. It is much more difficult to persuade someone to buy silicones if they have never bought them because they don't need them. That said, Dow Corning, a manufacturer of silicones recognized that a significant proportion of the market was looking for a transactional purchase. These were price-conscious companies wanting silicones without the technical advice and the premium support from Dow Corning. It took the brave step of setting up a new company called Xiameter, which met the needs of the transactional buyers as long as they purchased through the Xiameter website. In this way it met the needs of the premium buyers with its traditional Dow Corning offer as well as the needs of the price-conscious buyers with its new Xiameter offer (Gary, 2005). It is a rare step to have taken for a business to business company and for this reason has become a business school case study (Kashani and Francis, 2006).

Charge more

The secret of high profitability is often associated with high prices. High prices can only be sustained if a product is thought to be worth it. High prices which are simply overcharging will be recognized as a rip-off and eventually the company will lose out. It is possible to obtain higher prices for a product by differentiation and branding. They often go together. In fact, *Forbes* reports that '86 per cent of buyers will pay more for a better customer experience' (Crandell, 2013).

Differentiation means making your offer different. Even the most basic proposition differs when offered by two separate companies. Each company employs a diversity of people who have their own inimitable way of dealing with customers. Each company will have special terms and conditions. They most probably have dissimilar service levels. These differences can matter and may justify different prices to some people. This example is merely to point out that there are always differences between companies even if they sell the same products. Pulling out these differences and making them special is the art of good marketing. The marketing should create a greater appreciation for the brand and may well justify a premium price.

If there are significant differences in service features such as extended price warranties, quicker deliveries and a loyalty programme, we can see that a price premium could easily be justified. If the brand is strongly promoted with a clear and distinct message, it too could be used to justify a higher price. As long as the higher prices are attached to a greater number of perceived benefits, the product will stay on the value equivalence line. Only if the benefits are thought to be insufficient against the price will the company be under threat of losing market share.

Sell more

Selling more product isn't easy. It isn't as if there is a tap that can be turned on to sell more product. It is sometimes possible to sell more by lowering the price. However, lower prices mean lower margins and may mean lower profits unless compensated by a larger volume of sales. B2B markets are often relatively inelastic, in that a drop in price does not always result in a large increase in sales. People only need so many widgets to build into the product they are making. They don't buy and consume widgets for their own sake. Selling more products in B2B markets is seldom about simply lowering prices. We have been taught that success in business to business markets is about getting the marketing mix in tune with customers, which is making sure they have the right product, at the right price, in the right place, with the right promotion.

Or is it? In 2013, Richard Ettenson, Eduardo Conrado and Jonathan Knowles wrote an article in the *Harvard Business Review* entitled 'Rethinking the 4P's' (Ettenson *et al*, 2013). They argued that the 4P model is not suited to the B2B world. They claimed that the old 4P framework stresses product technology and quality. These, they said, are hygiene factors and do not differentiate. In an attempt to shift the focus from products to solutions, they suggested the SAVE framework. SAVE is an acronym for solution, access, value, and education:

- **Solution** (rather than Product). This places the emphasis on solving the problem rather than selling the product.
- **Access** (rather than Place). It is important to have access to customers wherever they are and whatever they are doing. This means that bricks-and-mortar distribution outlets are far less relevant today than, for example, the internet.
- **Value** (rather than Price). People care far less about the price than what they get for their money – it is value that matters.
- **Education** (rather than Promotion). Promotion can be seen as manipulative and in many B2B markets, trust and reputation are more important. Trust is built up over time in an educative way.

This focus on solutions is important in business to business markets. People don't buy products for their direct consumption and enjoyment as they do in consumer markets. Products (and services) are bought to meld with all the other purchases and are transformed into a new offer, which is sold into the value chain. Even if you lower the price people may not buy more, because they can't – they are limited by how many widgets are needed in whatever they are making. All the lower prices will do is destabilize the market and encourage a price war with competitors.

More than anything else, B2B customers want suppliers that can help them achieve their goals. They want suppliers that are proactive with solutions. They want to deal with a company that is seamless in the way it does business, especially with those factors that are crucially important. This adds up to a great customer experience for most business to business companies. Price linked to a great solution means value. Good value is associated with great customer experience and it drives sales.

Keeping track of prices

Customer experience professionals spend less time thinking about the effect of price than other elements of the marketing mix. Product, promotion and channel get far more attention. Price is such an important part of the offer and should be high on every customer experience manager's agenda. The pricing subjects we need to keep track of are:

Customers' perceptions of price: we need to understand whether customers see price in isolation or whether they measure cost in use. The price of a Scania truck may seem more expensive than some other brands but not when it is measured against its reliability, its lower depreciation, lower lifetime costs, etc. However, not all fleet managers measure the lifetime value of the truck. As is often the case, segmentation may be the answer – finding people who comprehend and seek lifetime value. Understanding how companies perceive price helps us find opportunities to sell more value and build stronger customer experience.

Bundling versus menu pricing: some people like a holiday where everything is included and others prefer to pay separately for the hotel, the airline, the food and the drink. So it is in business. Some people are happy to buy a bundle of products and services from one company and others want the flexibility of buying from multiple sources. Again, we must understand the different requirements of customers so that we can satisfy their pricing needs.

Competitors' prices: there is no getting away from it, customers are becoming more aware of prices from a wide range of suppliers. It is not unusual for a B2B buyer to challenge their incumbent supplier and say that a competitor has a significantly lower price. However, the competitor's offer may not be exactly the same. The products could be slightly different, warranties could be different, technical advice may not be included, delivery may be longer, the new supplier may not stay in the market for long. In an attempt to drive prices down, the customer may fail to fully explain differences between the offers. In order to achieve good customer experience, we need to be constantly reminding customers how and why our offer is better than that of the competition, even if our prices are higher.

Things to think about

- Where do your company and products fit on the value equivalence line? Are you to the left of the line and need to increase the perceived benefits of your offer? Are you to the right-hand side of the line at a point where you can continue to win market share or where you can raise prices and increase profitability?

- How transparent are your prices? How transparent are the prices of your competitors? How high are industry margins?

- To what extent do your prices and margins make you vulnerable to a disruptor?

- How do your customers understand value – what do they look for?

- What are the opportunities for improving customer perceptions of the value of your offer?

References

CNBC (2017) Meet the 2017 CNBC Disruptor 50 companies [Online] available from: www.cnbc.com/2017/05/16/the-2017-cnbc-disruptor-50-list-of-companies.html [last accessed 3 October 2017]

Crandell, C (2013) Customer experience: Is it the chicken or the egg? *Forbes*, 21 Jan [Online] available at: https://www.forbes.com/sites/christinecrandell/2013/01/21/customer-experience-is-it-the-chicken-or-egg/#7b50ab3a3557 [last accessed 3 October 2017]

Ettenson, R, Conrado, E and Knowles, J (2013) Rethinking the 4P's, *Harvard Business Review*, January/February

Gary, L (2005) Dow Corning's Big Pricing Gamble, *Harvard Business School Working Knowledge*, 3 July [Online] available at: https://hbswk.hbs.edu/archive/dow-corning-s-big-pricing-gamble [last accessed 3 October 2107]

Kashani, K and Francis, I (2006) *Xiameter: The past and future of a 'disruptive innovation'*, *Harvard Business Review* Case Studies, Harvard Business Publishing, Boston, MA

McAlone, N. (2015) This man invented the digital camera in 1975 – and his bosses at Kodak never let it see the light of day, *Business Insider UK* [Online] available from: http://uk.businessinsider.com/ [last accessed 3 October 2017]

Place and its role in creating better customer experience

Customer experience in the marketing channel

Many business to business companies are not suitably equipped to serve their markets. They may be too geographically distant from them. They may lack the necessary distribution points to reach customers. They may be very good at producing business products and prefer to leave the marketing and distribution to someone else who is better at it.

'Place' or, more aptly, 'distribution', is the means by which products and services are moved through the value chain. It is not unusual in business to business markets for a product to move through different channels within the value chain. For example, business to business companies cherish large accounts and want to look after them personally. These large accounts are usually supplied direct. Medium and small accounts may be serviced by a mix of wholesalers and stockists. Increasingly business to business companies are offering their products online.

Variations in B2B supply chains are illustrated in Figure 17.1.

Managing customer experience in distribution can be a challenge. When a customer is remote, the supplier may not have control of the customer touch points. Unless the stockist is exclusive to one manufacturer, it is likely to offer a choice of different brands and there is nothing to stop it choosing to push a competitive product. Distributors are very often the channel 'captain', enjoying the biggest margin in the value chain and determining whose product is presented to the customer. Of course, distributors are very variable. Some are active in pushing certain brands while others act more as distribution depots leaving the brand specification to their customers.

Figure 17.1 Options in B2B supply chains

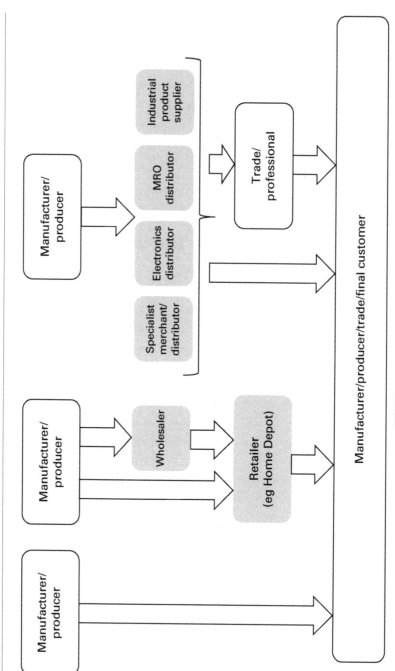

We have seen in the previous chapter that distributors add a significant amount to the price of products for the services they offer. This makes them targets for disrupters. However, distributors aren't an unnecessary expense, they provide real and valued services. Let us examine the different types of business to business distributors and their roles.

The logistics of distribution

Direct

The simplest form of distribution for a business to business company is direct to the customer. The automotive industry and other assembly industries buy direct and require just-in-time (JIT) deliveries. Assembly lines need the right components in the right quantity at the right time. The assembly companies do not have sufficient warehouse space to keep all the components in stock and require their suppliers to deliver products at a precise time. Some companies have become so dependent on just-in-time deliveries that the experience of an on-time delivery has become the essential standard. If something conspires to prevent the delivery arriving on time, the consequences could be dire. Failure to receive vital components may result in stopping a production line and the stockpiling of other components that are delivered as part of the sophisticated assembly plan. It points to the importance of making sure that any dependency that exists between the supplier and customer is totally respected.

Own depots

In the past many manufacturing companies had their own depots which acted in a similar way to the merchant outlets supplying local customers. As one would expect, these manufacturer-owned outlets did not sell competing products. They faced two disadvantages, which have resulted in them declining in importance. From the manufacturer's point of view it was often difficult for depots to be financially viable through the sales of a single brand. From the customer's point of view there was limited choice because the depots sold only one brand.

These manufacturer-owned outlets still exist in the distribution of industrial gases and welding equipment but they are becoming rarer as cost savings push distribution into the hands of independent merchants.

Maintenance, repair and operations (MRO) distributors

MRO distributors are companies that sell to any company (and also to the general public) often through a catalogue or over the internet. Examples of such companies in the US are W. W. Grainger and McMaster-Carr, and in Europe RS Components and Premier Farnell. These companies have developed into suppliers of products for maintenance, repair and operations (MRO).

Suppliers of electronic bits and pieces also figure as important MRO companies. Some distributors specialize just in electronic products. They include large catalogue companies such as Avnet, Arrow and Future Electronics. Their principal value proposition and claim on customer experience is product choice. Some of these companies carry hundreds of thousands of different products.

Merchants and stockists

Many business to business products are routed through merchants. These companies carry a wide range of products usually limited to those required by a particular trade – electricians, plumbers, hairdressers, pharmacists and the like. They have local showrooms and delivery vans, which will drop off orders, even those placed the same day.

Merchants stock and deliver almost everything. They supply drugs to chemists, food and drink to restaurants, health and safety products to factories, janitorial products to offices, chemicals to formulators, paper to printers. If a product is regularly consumed in the value chain, it almost certainly provides opportunities for merchants. In the construction industry, for example, they provide building materials and tools for customers who can drop into the outlet or receive daily deliveries.

Merchants provide local stocking points for customers. Printers have very little storage space. They buy reams and pallets of paper almost every day and prefer to receive the delivery first thing in the morning so that they have the paper for that day's printing schedule. It is physically impossible for paper merchants to deliver to every printer between 8 am and 9 am each day as most printers would wish. This means that they have to carefully manage customers' expectations. If the printer isn't going to use the paper for a couple of days, it may be possible to schedule the delivery for a more manageable time and not that early morning slot that is coveted by most customers. It may be possible for the paper merchant to manage consignment stock, in which the paper supplies are stored at the printers and only charged when drawn from the stock. In the case of printers, the customer experience from their paper merchant is significantly influenced by its ability to deliver on time. In fact, it is the deliveries that influence the customer experience as the paper that is sold by the merchants is the same almost everywhere. In such a situation, with frequent deliveries, the driver of the delivery van becomes the face of the paper merchant. The attitude of the driver in terms of their willingness to help unloading and moving paper into the printers has a big bearing on customer experience for the merchant.

The best distributors are very often the mom-and-pop companies, privately owned and dependent on their local customers. If a customer runs out of stock on Christmas Eve, the distributor thinks nothing of staying late to sort out the problem. These mom-and-pop distributors have been gobbled up by larger groups who have benefits of scale and an ability to provide customers with a service over a much larger footprint. This is not without problems as one of our contributors to the book (a distributor) told us:

'We have grown through acquisition. We have bought a number of small-to medium-size distributors all with a fantastic service ethic. It is why they were successful. They would go to the ends of the earth for their customers. However, they did it in their own inimitable ways. We are a large organization and have to do things differently. We are more planned and structured in what we do. These small mom-and-pop distributors find it really difficult doing things our way. They don't think that our service levels are up to what their customers expect. Our challenge is to provide excellent customer experience in a consistent way rather than allowing customer service anarchy – even though this anarchy can include some fabulous examples of service delivery.'

Retailers

We shouldn't forget that the lines between business to consumer and business to business companies are becoming increasingly blurred. In the construction industry there are many small businesses that require tools and equipment and find it just as convenient to buy from DIY superstores such as B&Q (in the UK) or Lowes and Home Depot (in the US). Historically tradespeople have shunned these outlets in the belief that they are not set up to serve professional construction workers. To that extent, the customer experience for the professional at the DIY store was lacking. However, such is the opportunity for serving trade customers, the DIY stores now have separate entrances, reserved parking and dedicated checkouts for the pros. The DIY stores have upped their game and responded with a more appropriate customer experience for the professional.

Customer experience in the B2B channel

Whatever their speciality, these merchant and distribution companies are a form of logistics outsourcing. They offer services that manufacturers find hard to provide. They live and die by their ability to look after customers and their every need.

Although channel partners are not under the direct control of the product supplier, they are still able to deliver excellent customer experience. David Ross in his book *The Intimate Supply Chain* (Ross, 2008), describes these services:

Selling and promoting: the sales function can be difficult for producers, especially managing sales to relatively small companies spread across a wide geographical area. Wholesalers and distributors have local knowledge. They use this knowledge to tailor promotional campaigns, product offerings, quick delivery and credit to companies within their radius of supply. This may incur the merchant extracting a significant margin of 25 to 33 per cent but, by buying in bulk with heavy discounts, these margins enable them to offer a price to the customer that is within acceptable bounds.

Offer choice: customers love choice. This is a double-edged sword to a manufacturer using distributors as they have to fight for shelf space against competing brands. Obtaining a premium position at distributors can be bought. Higher margins and bonus schemes can push products to the front. However, such strategies offer no guarantee of excellent customer experience. Far better to work with channel partners helping them provide local promotions or training for the people on the merchants' sales desk. There may be opportunities to develop point-of-sale displays that show off products in merchant outlets and help the customer get closer to them.

Information: people using merchants and stockists often seek advice. They want information on the products they are buying and their suitability for the job to be done. Merchant customers are interested in new products. They want to know about better ways of using the products. The distribution channel is a perfect opportunity to provide this, with wall charts, leaflets and trained sales agents.

Customer orientation: merchants are by their very nature attuned to the needs of customers. They open their outlets early and close them late. They have people available to answer the phone, take orders and deal with enquiries. They are in the business of selling rather than making and so they understand service better than manufacturers. It isn't unusual for a merchant to provide its customers with a seating area with newspapers and coffee on tap. This experience is unlikely to be found in many manufacturing companies.

Payment options: manufacturers, especially large corporates, are suspicious of small customers. They have draconian credit requirements, which they readily impose when a customer goes over the limit. A merchant is likely to be more sympathetic. They have local knowledge. They may use discretion in flexing the payment options so that a customer is helped out over a temporary difficulty and is forever grateful and loyal.

Small quantities: manufacturers and large companies dislike small orders. They excel at long production runs, volume sales and dealing with big customers. However, small customers can be profitable and merchants are happy to break bulk into small quantities and charge appropriately. The customer who wants a small quantity (often for a quick job) appreciates the service and is happy to pay the premium price.

In spite of their customer centricity, distributors face challenges in delivering excellent customer experience. Most distributors supply the market through multiple outlets, each run by a small team with a manager. Traditionally their performance has been rewarded on sales revenue. Distributors have woken up to the importance of the Net Promoter Score®, and nowadays, the managers' performance on this metric may be built into the remuneration package. The manager is the person that makes the difference.

Contributors to our book had a good deal to say on this subject.

> 'We see branches that get a new branch manager. The old one made losses and the new one focuses on customer experience and it turns into profit. We still have a lot to do in terms of recruiting the right people. Understanding the profile of people that suit customer experience is difficult. We used to reward people for things that now we don't want them to do. If you drive sales, that's all that you will you get. It may mean that in order to achieve the sales the branch reduces prices. Then, the next time the customer orders from that branch, they are disillusioned because the price has gone up.'

'The harder challenge is going to be on the commercial guys because they have a culture of buying and selling – being opportunistic with customers. There is a culture of trying to squeeze profitability depending on how prices are going. When a salesperson sees that a product is short he is going to screw as much as he can for that particular product. It's in their DNA and it's what their bonus incentivizes them to do. They get a pat on the back if they're successful at selling more. If we start saying "hang on a minute and take care of your customer and make sure each gets the best deal to get some long-term loyalty", I think most of our guys would jump for the short term.

We have started incentivizing around Net Promoter Score®. It's at a higher level. The sales guys still are incentivized by gross profit and margin. We've just started putting NPS as a KPI and it's just a start. We need to try and drive the behaviour towards experience and see where it goes.'

Merchant trends

Merchants take customer experience very seriously indeed. Every large merchant group regularly measures customer satisfaction and Net Promoter Scores®. Whereas manufacturers in B2B markets achieve NPS of between 20 and 30, merchants often have NPS scores of 50 or more.[1] They have the people in the store who can offer the personal touch. They have become the front-line staff of the manufacturers. It is not surprising that merchants are growing in importance. We can expect this trend to continue.

In the past, merchants rewarded their staff according to their sales performance. This yielded results but it also created longer-term problems. The sales push was usually associated with a temporary offer such as discounts. Inevitably these have an effect on profits and discounts cannot continue forever. Today's merchants reward their staff on customer experience metrics such as the Net Promoter Score®. A customer that achieves a great experience today will come back again and again to enjoy that experience in the future – without a discount.

Other trends are taking place in distribution channels. The seamless experience that customers so much appreciate when buying from a merchant will become even more important. Customers now expect to buy online and pick up the product in the store. Whereas manufacturers have been slow to develop their online offer, merchants have embraced it.

In the customer's eyes the manufacturer and merchant divide is becoming blurred. Customers want to buy the product from the merchant and, if it doesn't suit or is faulty, they want to return it to the merchant. Products that used to be sent to manufacturers for servicing are likely to be dropped off at the merchant in the future. The merchants of tomorrow will be offering seamless customer experience across all customer touch points.

Merchants have the advantage of dealing with customers at the point of sale. This means that they can pick up a good deal of granular data on their customers. The data can be mined to ensure that customers receive targeted, timely and relevant information. This customer data is unlikely to be passed back to the manufacturer. Knowledge is power and the merchants will increase that power in future years.

Digital marketing and B2B customer experience

Customers are looking for a seamless and effortless way of doing business. Many business to business companies are still stuck in a groove that requires their customers to buy from one channel only. They have a salesforce that wines and dines customers and a customer service centre that takes the orders. Prior to 1990 retailers served their customers with a physical store or a catalogue, which the customer could visit to view the goods and place an order.

Things have changed in B2C markets. Retailers now offer customers a variety of options for doing business. Physical shops are still important. Most retailers now offer their goods and services from their websites. Customers can phone and place orders. This is omnichannel marketing. Customers want the choice and expect it. It is part of the seamless experience that enables customers to buy products effortlessly.

Business to business companies are waking up to omnichannel marketing. Merchants supplying tools and equipment have embraced all the channels and their customers can call in at a store, buy online or phone with an order. Other B2B companies are finding it more challenging. They face complex buying situations. Some customers are huge and have multiple decision-makers, others are small and the decision-making unit is much simpler. Big customers get special treatment and are supplied direct while smaller ones may have to buy through stockists. Depending on who is buying, a B2B supplier's prices can vary enormously.

According to Forrester Research in 2015, just over 10 per cent of all B2B sales in the US were predicted to be via e-commerce in 2017 (eMarketer, 2016). It is a small proportion of total B2B sales but growing at 6 to 8 per cent per annum. Compared to B2C retailers, B2B e-commerce is not very sophisticated. Many B2B companies lack the IT nous to serve the complex range of customers with an e-commerce channel.

Having successfully disrupted and changed attitudes to e-commerce among B2C retailers, Amazon is now turning its attention to B2B markets. Amazon Business provides a platform for companies selling computers, office equipment, power tools and janitorial supplies. They offer the ability to vary discounts for the volume of transactions and the flexibility to tailor offers to the needs of different business customers. We can expect this to have a significant effect on B2B omnichannel marketing over the next few years.

Things to think about

- Which channels do you use to reach the market at the present? Which channels are favoured by your customers?
- What do customers look for from the channels they use? To what extent do they get what they are looking for?
- What access do you have to these distribution channels? How could you change the emphasis on them, should you need to do so?
- What can you do for your distribution partners that will help them sell your products and give customers a better experience?
- How do you segment your customers – is it on the basis of their size or their industry or can you recognize differences in their behaviour and needs?
- How could a different approach to segmenting your customers improve customer experience?
- What is your success at omnichannel marketing? How can you improve your digital offer?

Note

1 See B2B International's website (www.b2binternational.com) for benchmarks on NPS.

References

eMarketer (2016) B2B Ecommerce Market Is Still Maturing [Online] available from: https://www.emarketer.com/Article/B2B-Ecommerce-Market-Still-Maturing/1014311 [last accessed 11 November 2017]

Ross, DF (2008) *The Intimate Supply Chain: Leveraging the supply chain to manage the customer experience*, CRC Press, Boca Raton, FL

Promotion and its role in creating better customer experience 18

The changing role of promotions

The term promotion has a number of meanings. To some it means 'money back' offers. It can mean any activity that supports a cause. In this chapter we use the term as a catch-all to embrace the different means of communicating with customers and potential customers to publicize a company's offer. A significant proportion of promotion is advertising, which can be in print, or digital on websites or banners online. Promotions in business to business marketing are also likely to include direct mail, public relations, exhibitions, seminars and the like.

The purpose of promotions is to stimulate interest in an offer by building awareness, creating intrigue and hopefully driving some form of action. Successful promotions move the offer to a higher or more important position in the mind of the customer or potential customer. Done successfully, promotions can elevate the customer experience.

The purpose of promotions has always been to sell an idea or product. Promotions work has changed over time, adjusting to the conditions of the day. The earliest promotions were factual. They showed the product and described it – 'Drink Coca-Cola, delicious and refreshing'. Today promotions are more likely to play upon the emotions – 'Taste the feeling', 'Share a Coke with…'. In this more sophisticated role, promotions seek to fit products to lifestyles and aspirations. They have moved on from simply saying 'I am here, buy me!'

We are bombarded by promotions. They are at the side of the road as we drive to work. They jump out at us from our internet searches. They fill magazines and break up TV viewing. Because they are everywhere, we become inured to them. We are never quite sure to what extent they are reaching our consciousness. Do we switch off and filter out promotions that are not relevant? If we are not in the market for buying a car, does our brain filter out the adverts or is there some sort of subliminal impact we are unaware of?

Jay Walker-Smith of marketing firm Yankelovich says 'We've gone from being exposed to about 500 ads a day back in the 1970s to as many as 5,000 a day today' (Johnson, 2006). The estimate of the 5,000 exposures per day (some say even more) includes *any* exposure we may have to a brand, whether it is walking through the grocery store, noting a label on an item of clothing or looking at the contents of our fridge. If we focus just on the adverts rather than the brands, the number we see each day is estimated to be around 300 and we take note of just less than half of these (Johnson, 2014). Without getting too hung up on the figures, the message is clear, we are hit by a huge number of promotions every day and we are exposed to more brands than ever before. This explosion is testament to the effectiveness of promotions. Smart money wouldn't be spent on them if they didn't work.

Promotions do work. The more we tell people about our goods and services, the greater the chance they will buy them. Even so, we are still uncertain how the ads work despite a good deal of research. In fact, we haven't moved a great deal forward since John Wanamaker, the department-store magnate, made the comment more than 100 years ago that, 'Half the money I spend on advertising is wasted; the trouble is, I don't know which half' (Wikipedia, 2017).

The emotional connection with B2B suppliers

The role of emotions in business to consumer marketing is well-known and much talked about. Brands carry immense value. They reflect status. They imply membership of a certain group of like-minded people. They suggest the buyer is discriminating in some way. Even if we think that our emotions are under control and we personally are immune to the influence of brands, we are fairly certain that they are effective in influencing other people.

There is a natural suspicion that brands are a superficial layer upon products that are often quite similar. Sometimes, the only difference is the brand. Many of the products are made to the same specification in the same factory. It doesn't stop people believing in brands.

We may think that business to business buyers have a more rational frame of mind, after all, they are buying not for themselves but for their companies. This would be to deny the anxiety business to business buyers have about the decisions they make when choosing suppliers. Brands provide an emotional connection, which builds confidence. The promise that a brand makes prompts people to choose it. A business to business buyer relies on that promise. Their purchasing decision involves a high degree of risk. If they choose badly, their purchase could cost the company a good deal of money and it would certainly reflect badly on the buyer. The business customer relies on a strong emotional connection to help overcome this risk. It plays to the old adage 'No one ever got fired for buying IBM'. At the time the statement was created, in the late 1970s, IBM was the market leader in computers and always considered the 'safe bet'.

Research sponsored by Google looked at 3,000 B2B buyers and concluded that they are significantly more emotionally connected to their suppliers than people who buy consumer products (Nathan and Schmidt, 2013). They found that B2B buyers are 'almost 50 per cent more likely to buy a product or service if they see personal value in doing so'. The research that we have carried out in business to business markets fully supports Google's findings about the significant influence of emotions among B2B buyers. In our judgement, emotions may account for up to half the reason for choosing a certain B2B supplier even though this may not be understood or recognized by buyers themselves. We say this because we know that the majority of buyers of business to business goods and services have used the same suppliers for years. Over the years these companies must have been tempted to move to someone touting a more generous offer and have decided to stay loyal. They have looked the offers in the face and said 'we will stick with the brands we know thank you very much'.

Promotions that excite

Nowadays there is a need for promotions to stand out if they are to be successful. In consumer markets some adverts grip a nation. Returning to Coca-Cola, their adverts at the start of the Christmas season have become part of the Christmas ritual indicating the onset of festivities. At the same time John Lewis, the famous department store in the UK, launches its two-minute TV advert in the form of a short Christmas film, usually a tearjerker. In the US, the Super Bowl provides an opportunity for television commercials to hit over 100 million viewers. These aren't 30-second commercials – they are short films of high quality with surreal humour and special effects. The $4–$5 million slots on these major occasions are taken by brands, such as Budweiser, Coca-Cola, Doritos and GoDaddy. These promotions deliver an emotional promise. They excite to the point that the Super Bowl commercials on YouTube have been watched over 8 million times and the John Lewis ad, *Buster the Boxer*, has been watched more than 25 million times since November 2016.

In the 1980s and 1990s Benetton used promotions to shock and provoke people. Many of their campaigns had nothing to do with clothes. They talked about issues that were uncomfortable to many people – subjects such as HIV and hunger. They featured adverts with dramatic photographs, which included three human hearts and US president Barack Obama kissing Hugo Chavez, the former president of Venezuela. The campaigns divided audiences but then Benetton was not aiming at everybody, it had its eyes on the target market of 18-to-34-year-olds. Among those who liked the promotions it aimed to communicate the theme of 'united' by different colours, no matter what race, culture or gender. As with everything, a campaign can run its course and Benetton have moved away from controversial themes to a more traditional approach, currently showing their products on female models of varied backgrounds and ages suggesting that the 52-year-old company has reached maturity.

Promotions, as we have described, become part of the customer experience of the brand. They are much discussed, often with heightened emotions among those that like and dislike them. It is unrealistic for business to business brands to promote in this way. Few B2B brands can afford TV commercials or address mass audiences. Business to business companies target buyers, technicians, production managers and company leaders. Most B2B promotions are still at the Neanderthal stage of advertising, 'here I am, please buy me'. B2B companies would worry about a strategy courting controversy. They may feel that a promotion aiming at emotions is too far off the mark for them.

However, B2B audiences are the same people who shed a tear or laugh out loud at some of those consumer ads. Their emotions may be different but they are there nonetheless. They are looking for partners who can help them grow their business. They want security for the company they work for and not just themselves. They welcome innovation because it promises the chance of gaining an edge over their competitors.

Making B2B promotions work

Customer experiences are interactions with a company. The viewing of an ad is just as much an interaction as a call from a representative. The ad creates perceptions and expectations of the company.

We have seen in earlier chapters that business to business companies are looking for suppliers that can help them grow their business. Relationships and responsiveness are critical. Promotions that fail in this regard will not serve the company well. This means that websites that load slowly will not carry the message of speed and efficiency. A website that is hard to navigate will not communicate a company that is easy to do business with. A website that is bereft of people will not suggest a company that is strong on relationships.

The design and content of promotions should have the customer experience mission in mind. What sort of expectations does the company want to create about its products, services, and support? A clear brief must be given to the marketers and communications specialists so that they can create a tone and content in the promotions that promises the right experience.

Six different business to business ads for an industrial company were tested. Each was laid out in a similar way. They had an engaging visual across the top half of the advert, below which was a headline and below the headline was the body copy. It was a classic layout with an arresting graphic to draw interest from the limbic system and a headline to hit the parietal lobe. This was followed by well-written copy, a signature (the logo) and a call to action on the bottom right of the page. The agency that created the ads had put a good deal of thought into the visuals.

Surprisingly, the advert that was significantly preferred in every way featured a photograph of a research and development boffin who stood next to his invention. The headline said 'Pure Genius'. The body text explained how the invention could benefit buyers of the product. The more creative treatments were blown away by a simple composition of the product and the person who had created it. It hit the emotional spot – it inspired viewers to believe that this invention could help their company gain a competitive edge.

Other ads that test well among business to business audiences are testimonials. A real-life customer that is prepared to be featured in an advert and praise a supplier is believable. Air Products, the industrial gases company, tested a number of different ads to see which would be best for promoting their brand. Amongst other things, Air Products sells gases for cryogenic purposes (freezing products) and one of the ads featured a young man who looked like an Arctic explorer in an Arctic environment. The dramatic picture drew people in. The headline was even more powerful. It said 'After years of living at –18° C Mark Williams knows how to create your ideal freezing system'. The ad went on to say that Mark Williams is an Air Products employee devoted to the cryogenic line of business and who is there to help. This testimonial, from an employee of Air Products who spends a good deal of his time working in freezing conditions, was very convincing.

Public relations

The term PR is used to refer to both public relations and press relations. They are close bedfellows and it is the press bit we want to comment on first. If you are reading a magazine, a journal or a paper and you see something in an article about one of your suppliers, you are likely to take note. It draws your attention and you may mention it to a colleague. Its impact could be such that you copy the article and circulate it to people you think may be interested. This action is more likely following sight of some editorial than if you spotted an advert. Because it hasn't been paid for (directly) it carries more credibility. Michael Levine, the author of *Guerrilla P.R.*, suggests that an article in a magazine is between 10 and 100 times more valuable than an advertisement (Levine, 2008).

Then there is the public relations side of things. In the B2B world this includes organizing sponsored events with speakers. An interesting subject, well-known speakers and a good location is a great recipe for attracting a B2B audience. It is likely that the people who attend such events will be advocates of the company. This means that there will be many a discussion among the delegates about the sponsor and much will be positive. As with the press comment, testimonials from a third party are so much more powerful. The goodwill and the relationships that can be built up by PR events such as this all contribute to the B2B experience.

Things to think about

- Who are your target customers and what emotions drive their choice of suppliers? How does this differ throughout your customers and their customer journeys?

- What promotions do you use to connect with target customers? What messages and emotions are communicated in these promotions?

- In what way could you change your promotions to gain a greater emotional connection with customers? What would excite your customers and potential customers?

- In what way do you think this improved emotional connection would improve customer experience?

References

Johnson, C (2006) Cutting Through Advertising Clutter [Online] available from: www.cbsnews.com/news/cutting-through-advertising-clutter/ [last accessed 3 October 2017]

Johnson, S (2014) New Research Sheds Light on Daily Ad Exposures [Online] available from: https://sjinsights.net/2014/09/29/new-research-sheds-light-on-daily-ad-exposures/ [last accessed 3 October 2017]

Levine, M (2008) *Guerrilla P.R. 2.0: Wage an effective publicity campaign without going broke*, Harper Business, New York

Nathan, S and Schmidt, K (2013) From Promotion to Emotion: Connecting B2B Customers to Brands [Online] available from: https://www.thinkwithgoogle.com/marketing-resources/promotion-emotion-b2b/ [last accessed 3 October 2017]

Wikipedia (2017) John Wanamaker [Online] available from: https://en.wikipedia.org/wiki/John_Wanamaker [last accessed 3 October 2017]

The role of people in creating better customer experience

19

What are relationships?

Asking the question 'what are relationships?' may seem a peculiar start to this chapter. We have been discussing relationships throughout the book. We know what relationships are. They are the bonds between a customer and a company.

By far the majority of relationships between customers and B2B companies comprise people. A range of different people may be involved. Salespeople talk to a wide cross-section of personnel at a customer. Customer service staff talk to procurement. Finance and administration staff connect with counterparts in similar roles at customers. Senior managers and directors may from time to time visit customers to meet their opposite numbers and to demonstrate how much their custom is valued. Technical staff from a supplier talk to production and technical people at the customer. There are many opportunities for relationships between B2B companies and their customers and most of them involve people.

If the contact between people at the customer and the supplier has existed for some time, friendships are created. Knowledge is built up about the personal agendas of customer personnel and a good deal may be known about each other's private lives. Relationships are crafted to the needs of different individuals. Some people within a customer may prefer a formal businesslike relationship while others thrive on banter about their personal interests. It is important to get the right balance.

A close relationship doesn't necessarily mean spending the bulk of time with customers gossiping or discussing sports. The customer, out of politeness, may indulge such conversations but most prefer these to be lubricants to the conversation rather than the centrepiece. The centrepiece should be how the two companies can work together to help the customer grow.

Intuitively we know that strong relationships are good but what effect do they have on a business? If strong relationships are linked to loyalty, and it seems likely that they are, this should be something we can measure. The amount of repeat business given to a company would be a good indication of a strong relationship. An article in *Harvard Business Review* in 2015 compared the value that could be attributed to loyalty with the value that could be attributed to brands (Binder and Hanssens, 2015). It did this by examining 6,000 mergers and acquisitions that took place throughout the world between 2003 and 2013. The acquired companies that were analysed had, among other measures, to put on their balance sheets the value of their brands and the value of repeat business generated from customers that were known in person. At the beginning of the decade the asset value of repeat customers (the measure of loyalty) was on average 9 per cent and at the end of the decade the value of repeat customers had risen to 18 per cent of assets. Over the same period the asset value of the brands of the acquired companies dropped from 18 per cent in 2003 to just 10 per cent in 2013. The value of relationships and brands had swapped places. The data imply that customer relationships (ie, loyalty) are rising in importance while the value of brands is declining. (It could of course indicate that acquirers of companies have moved from investing in businesses with strong brands to businesses with strong customer relationships.) The *HBR* authors suggest that the reason for this switch in importance in favour of customer relationships is that they offer big opportunities for cross-selling.

Building strong personal relationships in business to business companies

This chapter is about people and how they can foster great customer experience. Here are some thoughts as to how people can be used to build strong relationships in business to business companies.

People are key

On the mumsnet website there is a post discussing 'why can't I sack my cleaner?' (mumsnet, 2011). Much of the discussion centres on the difficulty of sacking someone with whom there is a close relationship. Even if money is tight or if the cleaner is thought to be deficient in their work, it is hard to sack them. Relationships with people are personal and full of emotions. We are not suggesting that it is permissible to use these emotions to hold onto a customer while in some way failing to deliver against their expectations, we are simply saying that strong personal relationships are more likely to build loyalty than those that do not involve people. At the end of the day, we do business with people we like.

Being helpful

Has your car ever broken down and you required roadside assistance? What a relief when the mechanic turns up and gets you on your way. Your customer will feel the same way about you if you can solve one of their business problems or offer them advice. Being helpful builds the 'favours department' with a customer. The customer is grateful and in your debt. Your debt has a value and its accumulation builds customer loyalty.

Integrated solutions

A company has many departments and each may be superb at what it does. However, if these departments are not joined together it is not helpful to customers. A customer facing a problem is put through to a brilliant department that cannot solve an issue. If the department passes the customer to another brilliant department that similarly is not able to help, the customer will be unfulfilled. Customers are not interested in speaking to superbly run departments; they want quick solutions to their problems.

A few years ago, Bain & Company surveyed 362 firms and found that 80 per cent believed they delivered a superior experience to customers. However, when they asked *customers*, only 8 per cent said they were receiving a superior experience (Allen *et al*, 2005). Many companies believe that because they have well-run departments, they have a customer-focused business. It is the seamless integration of departments that makes for good customer experience.

Companies that use people not automatons

We have all been subjected to automated telephone answering systems. Surely the companies that install these systems have themselves been frustrated by them. Perhaps they choose to believe the sales patter of the company selling the automated systems who no doubt will say that their solution is customer friendly. Perhaps they persuade themselves that the cost savings are worth it.

When a company thinks of reducing inventory stock, changing delivery patterns, reducing the number of customer service personnel or putting in an automated answering system, they should ask themselves 'what will my customers think of this?' Cutting out human beings can sometimes save money but in most business to business situations it destroys personal relationships and results in a diminished customer experience. It may cost money in the long run.

There are occasions were jobs can be performed better without the involvement of people and so improve customer experience. An FAQ (frequently asked questions) section on a website may save customers a good deal of time telephoning a company to get an answer to a problem. Genuine customer reviews on a website could save the customer the time and trouble of seeking references and be much valued. Automated text messages informing of the progress of delivery may be preferred to a phone call.

Before we get too excited and see these examples as great opportunities to save money and at the same time improve customer experience, we should remember that most of the robot solutions are 'as well as' not 'instead of' using people. FAQs are an obvious easy and valuable addition to a website – but there is nothing like a conversation with a well-trained engineer when you are suffering a difficult technical problem. A pop-up on the website that says 'people who have bought this also bought these' is good – but it is no substitute for a skilled customer service rep who can perform the same task by asking some carefully crafted questions. People like dealing with people.

Hiring the right people

Being nice is always a key ingredient in building strong relationships. Hal Rosenbluth believes that his company's rise to become one of the largest corporate travel companies in the US was in good part due to finding the right people (Rosenbluth and McFerrin Peters, 1992). He says:

> 'Tenet number one is look for nice people. The rest will fall into place.... In our selection process, kindness, caring, compassion, and unselfishness carry more weight than years on the job, an impressive salary history, and stacks of degrees.'

As with everything, we are looking for the right balance. Rosenbluth knows what he's talking about, especially in his line of business, which is corporate travel. In a completely different line of business, that of 'factoring', money is loaned to companies that are financially up against the wall. Factoring is often the last resort. Here it will be necessary to have compassion tempered with realism as there are sure to be one or two customers who, in desperation, don't declare everything about their outstanding invoices. Fair but firm may be added to the list of qualities for people servicing business to business sectors.

If you have the right people in the wrong culture, they will leave. If you have the wrong people in the right culture, you will have to ask them to leave. Finding the right people with a culture that supports service and who fit in with a company culture is key.

With the right people in place it is then necessary to ensure systems and processes that enable people to deliver an appropriate service. As our customer experience guru friend, Chris Daffy, says (Hague, 2017):

> 'It is no good having really nice people on the front-line who are trained to offer excellent service if, when they turn to use the IT system, it fails. So ask yourself, have you got the systems and processes in place and are they properly aligned to make sure that you are serving customers well?'

Training

We would expect people on the front line to have been recruited because they have the right attitude. They will also need training. Training ensures that people do things your way and the right way – every time. It ensures consistency and quality. It is not a one-off thing. It is not a matter of putting people through a training course and thinking 'good, that job is finished'.

Zappos looks very carefully at the cultural fit of its new hires. Cultural fit accounts for 50 per cent of the weight in its hiring criteria (Heathfield, 2017). Once employed by Zappos, the first three to four weeks are spent in the call centre learning how to respond to customer needs. When this is finished, the new hire is offered $3,000 to leave the company. This is to test their resolve as an employee and to see if they are committed to the goals and culture of the company. It should also be pointed out that executives within the company are expected to roll up their sleeves and return to the phones at any time when the call centre is busy. Throughout the year the recruits learn new skills, and 10 to 20 per cent of each department's time is spent on team building activities. This is to share and develop the core values of Zappos and ensure that everyone is engaged in the culture. Training at Zappos is not one day in a classroom.

Training front-line staff in customer experience needs to cover all the obvious things. They need to learn the importance of listening to customers, showing empathy with them and how to ask open-ended questions to find out what customers are really thinking. Front-line staff need skills training to recognize and manage customers' emotions. With the right training they can use the right words and body language to change customers' emotions. We recall working for a large manufacturer of food ingredients. Every year the company entered into a new contract for the next 12 months and this was thrashed out around a negotiating table. A customer requested that one of the sales people from the food ingredient company should be changed. The sales person was 6'6" tall and built like a professional boxer. His presence around the table intimidated the customer and was not helpful to negotiations (at least from the customer's point of view). In fact, he was a gentle giant but he hadn't learned the art of body language to soften his threatening appearance.

Supported by excellent training, a company's front-line staff need to be empowered. If they have understood a problem and have the trust of the customer, they should be given the authority to solve the problem. This requires support from the top. Leaders must be confident that their staff will make the right decisions for the company. The reason that front-line staff are not empowered is usually because senior people within a business worry that an employee's bad judgement could put the company's reputation at risk. Well-trained and empowered employees will almost always respect the authority that is given to them and work within given boundaries. The benefit to the company of an empowered employee is the fast resolution to a customer problem. A small yield and a quick solution to a disgruntled customer can turn them into a loyal customer for life.

The front line is the obvious place to start with training but it is equally important in the rest of the company. It is within the company that customer experience can get stuck. If people in the accounts department, on the production line, or who are responsible for training don't understand the principles of customer service, they may do their job but prejudice the customer experience. Departments within a company provide services to other parts of the company. These other departments are customers even though no money changes hands. The service ethic has to run right through the company. It is an inside–out process. Chris Daffy illustrates this in Figure 19.1.

Figure 19.1   Training and the inside–out process

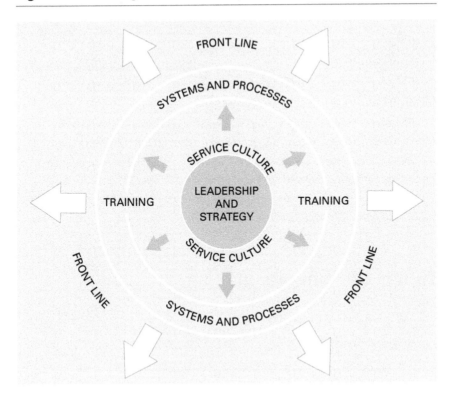

CASE STUDY   The Eddie Stobart story

In 1976 Eddie Stobart began a freight transport business in the UK with 8 trucks and 12 employees (Barford, 2011). Over four decades, helped by the original Eddie's son (also called Edward), the company has become one of the best-known logistics and road haulage companies in the UK with more than 2,200 trucks.

How did they do it?

Trucking is not a particularly glamorous business. At least, it wasn't until the Stobart family arrived. The young Edward, who was put in charge of the business, thought that the British haulage industry looked very unprofessional (*The Telegraph,* 2011). The company invested in new trucks that were always clean and polished. Each truck was personified with a female name on the lower part of the doors. In the early days of road haulage in the UK, drivers of trucks looked rough. Eddie Stobart drivers looked like they were going to work in an office. They wore a shirt and tie and were instructed to wave back and sound their horns when a member of the public acknowledged them.

Spotting Eddie Stobart trucks became a sport and soon there was a fan club. Today the fan club has 35,000 members. In most service stations around the country it is possible to buy Eddie Stobart toy trucks.

Eddie Stobart used people to bring customer experience to the mundane trucking business. The 'product' was freight movement but the differentiation and the customer experience came from the drivers and the personification of the trucks. Through the use of small but effective devices that differentiated the company he built a business which today has revenues of £550 million ($740 million) (*Logistics Manager,* 2017).

Things to think about

- How strong are the relationships between your staff and your customers?
- What is the contribution of your staff to the loyalty of your customers?
- To what extent are the departments within your company integrated to provide seamless customer solutions?
- When you hire people within your company (in any position) to what extent do you take into consideration their customer friendliness?
- What training do customer-facing staff receive in delivering excellent customer experience?
- What training does everyone in your company receive on service excellence?
- How empowered are your employees?

References

Allen, J, Reichheld, FF, Hamilton, B and Markey, R (2005) Closing the delivery gap: How to achieve true customer-led growth, *Bain & Company Insights* [Online] available from: http://www.bain.com/publications/articles/closing-the-delivery-gap-newsletter.aspx [last accessed 3 October 2017]

Barford, V (2011) How did Eddie Stobart become so famous?, *BBC News Magazine* [Online] available from: http://www.bbc.co.uk/news/magazine-12925163 [last accessed 3 October 2017]

Binder, C and Hanssens, DM (2015) Why strong customer relationships trump powerful brands, *Harvard Business Review*, 14 April [Online] available at: https://hbr.org/2015/04/why-strong-customer-relationships-trump-powerful-brands [last accessed 3 October 2017]

Hague, N (2017) Go Beyond In Customer Experience – A Conversation With Chris Daffy [Online] available from: www.b2binternational.com/publications/go-beyond-in-customer-experience-a-conversation-with-chris-daffy/ [last accessed 3 October 2017]

Heathfield, SM (2017) Find out the Ways Zappos Reinforces Its Company Culture [Online] available from: www.thebalance.com/zappos-company-culture-1918813 [last accessed 3 October 2017]

Logistics Manager (2017) Eddie Stobart flotation to fund e-commerce growth, *Logistics Manager*, 23 March [Online] available from: https://www.logisticsmanager.com/eddie-stobart-flotation-to-fund-e-commerce-growth/ [last accessed 3 October 2017]

mumsnet (2011) Why can't I sack my cleaner?! [Online] available from: www.mumsnet.com/Talk/housekeeping/1218135-Why-cant-I-sack-my-cleaner [last accessed 2 November 2017]

Rosenbluth, HF and McFerrin Peters, D (1992) *The Customer Comes Second and Other Secrets of Exceptional Service*, William Morrow and Company, New York

The Telegraph (2011) Edward Stobart Obituary [Online] available from: www.telegraph.co.uk/news/obituaries/finance-obituaries/8419820/Edward-Stobart.html [last accessed 3 October 2017]

PART FIVE
Controls that ensure the customer experience programme stays on track

Measuring the performance of customer experience initiatives

20

Tracking results

The world has gone measurement mad. We know that we are in tricky territory trying to measure customer experience as it is very much influenced by emotions. However, measurements are necessary if improvements are to be made on the grounds that, 'if you can't measure it, you can't manage it'. We need measurements to tell us if we are improving and where we can improve.

There is a strong analogy to be made here with measuring our health. Everyone uses some benchmark to keep track of their health and rightly so. Our health is important and it would be irresponsible if we didn't take note. The measures we use as an indication of our health may be as informal as judging how easy or difficult it is to climb a flight of stairs or noting the position of the hole when we tighten our belt. We may have a more formal health check with a visit to the doctor to test our cardiac system, measure our blood pressure and run some blood tests.

In measuring customer experience we are looking at the health of our organization. Politicians know this is important at a national level. The Office for National Statistics in the UK has had a remit since 2011 to measure the life satisfaction and happiness of the nation. Politicians want to know if the people they represent are content. In 2016 the 'life satisfaction' measure for the UK was 7.7 out of 10 (ONS, 2017). As an aside, it is worth noting that if this score was achieved by a company for the satisfaction of its customers, it would be considered moderate rather than very good. The score should be around 8.0 out of 10 or more before we can say that people are feeling really satisfied.

This measure at a point in time is valuable. It tells us where we stand. What is more useful is knowing whether the score is changing in any way. A score of 7.7 out of 10 and rising is a very different story to one that is declining. Two data points are worthwhile but we need a few more than this to confirm a trend. We need to use customer experience metrics to track where we stand.

Pulse or period?

We have talked a lot about the customer journey and the different touch points on it. Understanding the performance of your company at each of these touch points will show where improvements need to take place. This type of performance measurement of events has become popular; perhaps too popular. Every time we buy something from Amazon or park our car at an airport or take a holiday we may be asked 'how was it for you?' A lot of companies go further than this and seek to measure satisfaction after just one touch point. A salesperson calls and it is followed by someone asking for a performance rating. A delivery takes place and another survey is posed on this subject alone.

Three McKinsey consultants, Alex Rawson, Ewan Duncan and Conor Jones, wrote an article in *Harvard Business Review* entitled 'The Truth About Customer Experience' (Rawson *et al*, 2013). It explored the pros and cons of focusing on the measurement of narrow and single events rather than assessing the bigger end-to-end journey. The authors argue that the narrow view can give a distorted picture. A company may do a good job at one touch point on the customer journey, such as answering customers' calls. If this doesn't take account of what is happening elsewhere, it could miss out on the assessment of the reasons for the call and the root causes of any problem that necessitated the call.

The authors of the article believe that the answer lies in identifying key customer journeys and understanding a company's performance across that whole journey. This, they say, will show where and how to make improvements. In short, they think that a measurement on the performance of the journey can be more important than focusing on individual touch points.

It raises the question as to how often we should take a reading on customer experience performance. We know that emotions can sometimes fly into overdrive, especially if something critical hits the news. In the same way the customer satisfaction or loyalty score could be significantly influenced by a recent event – good or bad. Are we concerned about continuously feeling the pulse of the company or is an annual check-up preferred?

Annual measures on customer satisfaction allow time for any customer improvement initiatives to have an effect. They also ensure that customers aren't taxed with surveys every time they place an order. Too many surveys irritate customers especially if, after the survey, they can't see any obvious signs of improvement. Requests to take part in such surveys are quickly ignored. There are no hard and fast rules on the length of the interval between surveys, though once a year seems about right. It gives sufficient time for changes to feed through and it is not overburdening on customers.

When problems occur, a company would be blind or insensitive if these were to pass unnoticed. It is on such occasions that it makes sense to carry out research. For example, a company we work with could see that it was facing a problem with new customers. The company put all new customers through a credit check before orders could be placed. Following the credit check, only around a half of the newly acquired customers proceeded to place orders. Something was amiss. A deep dive on just 20 companies showed that the process of screening for purposes of credit checking was tedious and unfriendly. Signing on with other suppliers was much easier. The insights from this deep dive resulted in the company appointing a 'new product adviser' whose task was to look after these important new customer recruits. So successful was this initiative in motivating customers to start buying from the company that it wasn't long before another new product adviser was appointed. When problems occur, research should be carried out.

Social media as a source of customer experience

Twenty to thirty years ago market surveys were relatively novel. If you bought a new car and received a questionnaire asking what you thought of it, the chances are you would happily sit down for 15 to 20 minutes and complete the survey. Response rates were 70 to 80 per cent. Nowadays we are over-researched and response rates to customer surveys are in single figures. Business to business surveys can have their responses boosted by salesforces who beg their customers to complete the experience survey. This, in itself, can introduce a bias. Imagine that a salesperson says to the customer 'we are carrying out our annual customer feedback survey and it would be wonderful if you could find a few minutes to respond. If you could also find it in your heart to say something good about the service I have provided it would be very much appreciated.'

This causes us to think about other ways we can track customers' views on company performance in addition to the formal survey:

Track your mistakes: if you fail to do something for a customer, they will almost certainly be disappointed. You don't always have to ask to know that something is wrong. Internal metrics may be readily available. The number of complaints you receive, the number of occasions you fail to deliver on time and in full, the number of missed appointments, the number of returned products, all provide clues as to your performance.

Keep an eye on social media: at the present, most business to business companies have only a small number of Twitter followers and very little interaction on social media. However, social media is becoming more important for businesses and it is worth watching. Customers can leave reviews on a company Facebook page or Twitter feed. www.glassdoor.com provides a measure of how employees are treated. www.yelp.com was originally focused on restaurants and is pushing to become a review site for other industries. These media sites are sure to grow in importance and are worth watching.

Sentiment analysis: software is being developed that measures sentiment on subjects that are discussed on the internet. For example, we can use it to search for mentions of a company's name together with words that are classified as positive or negative. The software is improving all the time. It is getting better at ensuring that every time a name is mentioned, it really is the company under review and not a private individual or some other moniker. Kogan Page, the publisher of this book, has a number of valuable references on this subject (Grigsby, 2018; Struhl, 2015).

Information sources

Understanding customers has always been an imperative. According to the market research specialist, Walker, it will be even more so in the future. When they asked companies what actions or investments will have most impact on them in the years to 2020, 6 out of 10 respondents said 'understanding individual customer characteristics' (Walker, 2017).

The information sources that will provide this understanding of customer characteristics include purchase transactions, complaints and customer surveys. These data sources often exist in silos and need to be simplified and streamlined to create a better understanding. Purchase history resides with accounts, ordering information with customer service, sales calls and the discussions that take place are sometimes in the heads of the sales representatives. Bringing these data streams together is the role of the customer relationship management database.

Using a CRM system

Any company that is serious about customer experience needs a customer relationship management system (CRM). A CRM system contains a listing of all customers and potential customers, in which is recorded standard data such as the company contact details together with appropriate classifications such as its industry and size. In addition to this 'boilerplate' information on companies, specific details are kept on people who are decision makers or influencers. As a minimum this usually includes names of individuals, their titles, email addresses and telephone numbers. The CRM system allows additional data to be added such as individuals' ages, birth dates, sports interests, etc and purchasing history of the company. Some of this data may be useful for segmentation purposes. For example, companies can be given a grading such as platinum, gold, silver or bronze. If they have particular needs these can also be logged on the system.

As described, the CRM system is not much more than a sophisticated Excel spreadsheet. However, specialist CRM software is available for constant updating by customer service staff, salespeople and marketers, who can record interactions with customers and potential customers. These interactions typically include notes on sales visits, communications that have been sent, order details and deliveries, etc.

Customer lists and databases have always been vital to business to business companies, though not without challenges. Representatives often keep lists of their own customers and don't share updates with the rest of the company. The purpose of the CRM system is to centralize these ad hoc lists so that a master database is available for marketing and segmentation purposes. An up-to-date and fully fledged CRM is a mark of a customer-focused company. It is the means by which B2B companies communicate with current and future customers. A well-managed customer database demonstrates a commitment to customer knowledge, which is crucial for delivering customer experience.

We have described the management of customer databases as a vital tool for customer-centric business to business companies. It is surprising therefore how many companies have customer lists and CRM systems that are in disarray. The problem is caused by the mundane nature of managing the systems. Updating and cleaning contact details is boring, tedious and may be regarded as a low-level job so it is given to office juniors or an intern. This poor person may have little knowledge of the companies on the list and the dullness of the task means it is not kept in the pristine condition assumed by higher management. Salespeople can be notoriously neglectful in reporting changes that take place at their customers. They may keep to themselves up-to-date lists for sending out Christmas cards and dealing with their own precious customers.

It isn't unusual for CRM systems in large business to business companies to have a host of fields to complete that are ignored. Buoyed by enthusiasm to design a sophisticated system, the CRM is unwieldy from the start and is never updated. It is far better to start with a skeletal system that is easy to populate.

It is also important to keep the CRM system as clean as possible. The marketing department from time to time may purchase lists of prospective customers, which are loaded onto the CRM system. Many of the acquired company addresses are dead wood. The constant 'weeding' and maintenance of CRM systems is made all the more difficult as it gets loaded with junk. Before the purchased lists are loaded onto the CRM system they should be cleaned by the salesforce, with telephone calls to validate the contact details or a direct mail program to check for email bounce backs.

Drawing together the many strands of intelligence on customers and keeping these up-to-date in the CRM system is clearly important. The CRM system will provide an understanding of who the customers are, what they want, what they are buying and how they are being cared for. The CRM system is changing from being a technology resource to providing a critical tool for business strategy. Managed well, the CRM system will be a decision-making tool. It will provide an understanding of the customer that can be used proactively to serve the customer better through improved customer experience. This it will achieve by improvements such as:

- **Understanding customer needs**: providing insights on customer needs that can ensure they are better satisfied.

- **Communications with customers**: showing what customers want to know, how frequently they require communications and keeping track of how communications have affected their purchase activity.

- **Linking customer experience with sales and profitability**: using customer satisfaction and loyalty data to show how it is affecting sales volumes and profitability of customers.

- **Managing market share**: showing share of wallet and the customers that offer prospects for increased levels of business.

- **Managing churn**: managing lost customers by finding out who they are and why they are leaving.

- **On-boarding customers**: managing new customers to see how their sales are ramping up.

And finally, the maintenance of the customer database should bear in mind the General Data Protection Regulation (GDPR) that will be applicable in the European Union from May 2018. A discussion on the key points can be found in Chapter 13.

Things to think about

- What metrics do you have access to that show whether or not your customer experience performance is improving?
- How can you sense whether any new customer experience initiatives are working?
- Which non-survey metrics (such as social media) can you use as a measure of your customer experience performance?
- How would you judge the health of your CRM system? What is the quality of the data held on your CRM system?
- What is the link between your CRM system and customer experience?

References

Grigsby, M (2018) *Marketing Analytics: A practical guide to improving consumer insights using data techniques*, 2nd edn, Kogan Page, London

ONS (2017) Personal well-being in the UK: April 2016 to March 2017, *Office for National Statistics*, Statistical bulletin [Online} available from: www.ons.gov.uk [last accessed 3 October 2017]

Rawson, A, Duncan, E and Jones, C (2013) The truth about customer experience, *Harvard Business Review*, September

Struhl, S (2015) *Practical Text Analytics: Interpreting text and unstructured data for business intelligence*, Kogan Page, London

Walker (2017) Customers: The Future of B-to-B Customer Experience 2020 [Online] available from: www.walkerinfo.com/knowledge-center/webcasts/docs/Walker-Insights-Webcast-Customers-2020.pdf [last accessed 3 October 2017]

The challenge of continuous improvement in customer experience   21

Where to focus

We have reached the last chapter in the book but we haven't finished our work. In fact, it is a job that will never be finished. In the world of customer experience there is always more to be done. Fundamentals in customer experience are the six pillars. All six pillars must be in place in order to achieve customer experience. These are:

1 **Commitment:** a company must be fully committed to customer experience if it is to succeed and it is always best if this forceful commitment comes from the leaders of a company.

2 **Fulfilment:** customer experience must be more than a promise; it must deliver upon that promise. We call this fulfilment; doing what you say you will do.

3 **Seamlessness:** customers want to do business with companies that make life easy. This means the departmental silos that make up a company must be joined together in a seamless fashion with the objective of delivering customer experience.

4 **Responsiveness:** speed is of the essence when it comes to customer experience. Time is money. The internet and technology have set standards of quick delivery that businesses must meet.

5 Proactivity: customers don't think it is their responsibility to chase orders. They want to deal with companies who anticipate their needs and are proactive in meeting them.

6 Evolution: finally, expectations do not stay the same. What was acceptable yesterday has to be improved for today's customers. Customer experience needs to evolve constantly.

We have received great contributions from many people when collecting material for this book. Most of our contributors work in behemoths – large B2B companies that we call 'corporates'. They told us that they weren't there yet in delivering customer experience with consistency. They know that it is easier for small B2B companies to please their customers. Their owners think nothing of working late into the night or over the weekend to fulfil orders. In large companies the customer experience touches more people and is more complicated to deliver. They know that as large business to business companies they have a stronger hold on their customers than B2C companies. They know that in their companies not everyone has the same commitment to customer experience. They know that their task is made more difficult by the shackles of processes and bureaucracy.

This is not to say that a large B2B company can never deliver excellent customer experience. It is all down to the six pillars. It is about commitment and then fulfilment, seamlessness, responsiveness and proactivity. And finally, it is also about evolution.

We have seen that customer experience is achieved by a collection of very different tactics. Some are small and some are huge. They include things that are obvious, such as having the right product in the right place at the right price. They also include what may seem small and trivial things like smiling and saying 'thank you' to customers – but these things really matter.

The investment required in these actions, big and small, varies. It can cost a good deal to ensure that the right product is at the right place at the right price. It can be expensive to hire the right people. Equally, hiring the wrong people is costly and catastrophic for customer experience.

Some things cost very little and deliver a lot. Smiling and saying 'have a nice day' requires no investment and can achieve a good deal. While there is nothing wrong with a newsletter and a Christmas card, in themselves they will have only a marginal effect on customer experience.

The various actions that contribute towards customer experience in terms of their cost and what they can achieve are portrayed in Figure 21.1. Just as the pillars need to be in place, so do these tactics of customer experience delivery.

Figure 21.1   Investments versus outcomes in customer excellence

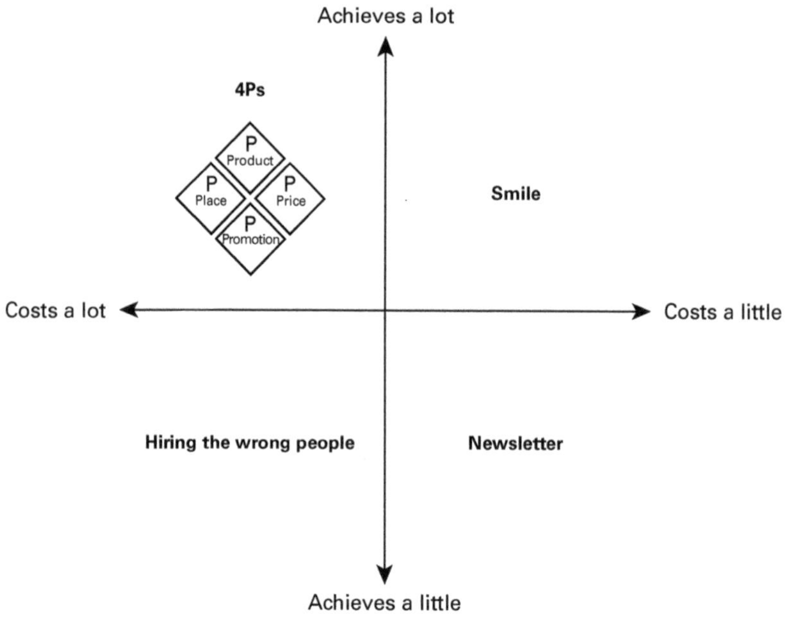

CX does not stand still

Strategies are not something that we change frequently. We set a course, we follow the course and we give it time to succeed. Everyone working towards the goal of customer experience should be aware of the strategy which, in its many variations, will have a similar theme such as 'to build loyal customers through always meeting expectations and beating them wherever possible'.

The overall strategy will be anchored and long term. From time to time there will be a need to make some changes to the strategic direction. This may be prompted by a need to improve customer satisfaction with certain groups of customers; the number of complaints could rise for some reason; there may be an urgent need to improve response times to enquiries.

While long-term strategies remain stable, at a tactical level there must be a good deal of fresh thinking. The things that excite people and generate good experiences today soon become everyday expectations. The personal effects that are laid out for us in hotel bathrooms were once so exciting we took them home. The hot cookie presented to us as we signed into our hotel no longer impresses. These things are still there but we expect more. This means that we need to continually refresh and improve our customer

Figure 21.2　The process of generating new customer experience

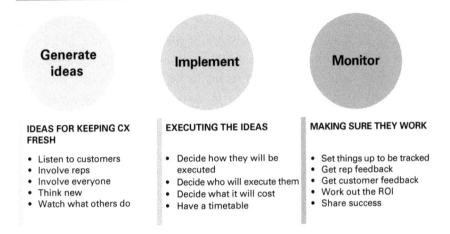

experience delivery. New ideas must be generated, implemented, monitored and judged. We will examine these three challenges for constant improvements in this final chapter. See Figure 21.2.

Generating ideas internally

There is and always has been a demand for 'cheaper, better, faster'. The unremitting appetite from customers for improvements to customer experience can be daunting because, at first pass, we are inclined to believe there must be a limit as to how far it is possible to improve on what are already excellent levels of performance.

The starting point for new ideas on customer experience must be to look right under our noses – to look for ideas from within our own companies. Sales representatives spend a lot of time with customers and are well placed to spot unmet needs. They have the opportunity to see how customers order products, modify them, how they work with them and how they store them in the warehouses. They see how competitors and other suppliers deliver excellent experiences to their customers. Sales representatives are therefore a first port of call for new ideas. Customer service reps and technical support teams talk to and visit customers. Just like the sales reps, they have antennae that pick up on ideas for new experiences.

In fact, everyone in an organization should be consulted. Steven Johnson, a specialist in innovation, makes the following point about generating ideas: *'It's not that the network itself is smart; it's that the individuals get smarter because they're connected to the network'* (Johnson, 2010). Johnson argues that the best way to generate ideas is to get everyone involved. An idea presented by someone in a workshop may spark another idea from someone else.

Procter & Gamble marshal the help of their 100,000-plus employees in innovating customer experience. They ask employees for new product ideas, opportunities for cutting costs, improving skills and making processes and policies more customer friendly (ClearAction, 2017). Someone in IT may more readily see an opportunity for making the customer experience quicker and seamless than a front-line salesperson.

Off-site venues for the ideation sessions can remove the day-to-day inhibitions that exist in many office environments. People who attend these sessions should be open-minded and creative. The moderator that leads the session should be inspiring and non-judgemental, encouraging everyone to suggest ideas no matter how crazy they seem. There will always be a later opportunity to screen the ideas in terms of their impact and practicality.

The aim is to arrive at as many ideas as possible of things that will achieve radical improvements to customer experience. The increasing demands for cheaper, better, faster may need a completely fresh view on how this can be accomplished (see Table 21.1).

Table 21.1   The relentless demands for improved experiences and possible responses

Increasing demands for...	Respond with...
Faster deliveries	Timed deliveries Overnight deliveries Consignment stock
More communications	Tweeted updates Emails (with purpose) Phone calls Hosted 'industry' events
Easier business transactions	Online ordering Subscription orders Telematic ordering
Financial savings	Extended product life Reduced service interval Improved productivity
Competitive opportunities	Consultancy for customers Ideation sessions for customers Trend analysis for customers

Little initiatives add up

'Cheaper, better and faster' aren't the only ways to deliver better experiences. A thoughtful action can mean a lot. The motivational trainer, Michael Heppell, calls these 'wee wows' (Heppell, 2015). We are reminded of one such event when we were working with a large supplier of food ingredients. The company had worked hard to win a customer in Northern Ireland. On the morning of the first bulk delivery a young woman accompanied the truck as it drove into the customer's plant. She introduced herself as a customer service representative and explained that although the customer may never see her again, she would always be at the end of a phone line to solve problems should they arise. She had made the trip to meet the customer especially to make this point. The customer never forgot it and grew to be one of the company's largest accounts.

These wee wows may be small but they are not trivial. A receptionist at a firm of business lawyers noticed that many clients visiting the company carried a Kindle or a book with them to while away time spent on trains, planes and in airports. It gave her the idea of creating a book club for clients. She asked colleagues which clients might be interested in the book club and generated a potential list of 50 members. Every two months she bought 50 copies of business books and sent them to the clients on the list. Every book was accompanied by a note that summarized thought-provoking points expressed in the books. The initiative cost $10,000 and ran for 12 months. In the following year the company sponsored 'insight nights' – evening sessions held at interesting venues where well-known luminaries made a half-hour presentation on their specialist subject and led a lively debate. In just a couple of years the lawyers positioned themselves as thought leaders, created lots of discussions and received numerous notes of gratitude.

Some wee wows are obvious but how many of us do them?

- Send cards of congratulation to clients when they get a promotion, when one of their kids graduates, when they have a baby, etc.
- Send a note to clients who have an anniversary with you as a supplier, simply to say thank you for your business over the last year, two years, etc.
- Invite a client to a sporting event. Send them a photo afterwards of everyone at the event.
- Phone the customer a few days after they have bought something to check that all is well.
- Buy cakes for your customers' staff.

These are not in any way intended to be the centrepiece of an excellent customer experience programme, they are simply small actions that can add delight.

Gifts we should not ignore

Business to business customers don't often complain (Beinhacker and Goodman, 2017). They have learned that in the process-driven environment of the B2B world it doesn't do any good. 'I am afraid that is the way we do things around here' is the anticipated reply. If the customer does complain, it is likely to be about the product, delivery problems, packaging or billing. It is seldom about sales support as the customer knows that it could damage their relationship with someone with whom they are in regular contact.

This means that when complaints are made they should be regarded as the tip of the iceberg and a gift. When addressed, there is likely to be considerable leverage of the positive virtuous spiral – an improvement in customer experience leading to greater loyalty, increased revenue and profits.

It is worth analysing the complaints to see the broad themes. Examining the complaint and its root cause should point to an opportunity for improvement. These could be about quality, delivery, sales service or accounting mistakes. In turn these broad themes can be analysed in detail. Quality complaints could be the failure to meet a specification, a product that fails in warranty, a product that doesn't perform adequately, one that doesn't last long enough, etc. Delivery complaints could be about failure to deliver on time, to deliver in full, failure to help unload and stock the product, delivery times that are too long, etc. The aim is to understand if there are specific areas of weakness that need to be rectified.

Complaints are a great source of ideas. When a genuine complaint is made it is by a customer that has cared to take the trouble to tell their story. We should be especially concerned about those companies that are dissatisfied but can't be bothered to complain. They are likely to take their business elsewhere without us knowing what we have done wrong.

Listening to customers

The internal view is only the starting point. We must extend our search for new initiatives and customers are an obvious hunting ground. Their expectations are changing all the time. An understanding of how they are changing and in what way will enable the CX programme to be modified to better meet new expectations.

Increasingly business to business customers buy more than products. They buy experiences together with products and services. They buy solutions. This is not only an opportunity to deliver a better customer experience with an extended offer, it is also an opportunity to generate additional revenue. There are usually more opportunities to build additional services and solutions than to make changes to the physical aspects of the product.

Collecting the views of customers can be on customer visits, through focus groups and surveys. Some business to business companies recruit a select group of customers to form a 'community' who are charged with feeding back ideas for improved customer service. The chosen customers are linked, sometimes joined on a software platform or simply attending events (as in the case of the legal company that ran 'insight nights'). The community's role is to provide reactions to customer experience initiatives and to keep their eyes and ears peeled for new initiatives that could be appropriate. It isn't necessary to have many people in this community, a dozen or a couple of dozen will be sufficient to give honest feedback.

A good idea is worth copying and they are happening all around us. There is no shame in copying or adapting other people's good ideas. If a text from the taxi you have ordered seems like a good idea, it may prompt a similar system for your customers. If you have been impressed by the music and soundtracks while held waiting on the phone, this could be something that would impress your customers.

Prioritizing the ideas

Not all ideas for freshening the customer experience will be of equal merit. Armed with lots of ideas, they must be sorted to determine which are worth pursuing. Prioritizing the ideas can be achieved using a simple scoring method in which each idea is given a rating out of 10 in terms of ease of implementing and the impact on the customer. They can be plotted on a matrix that indicates which are worth pursuing (see Figure 21.3).

Executing new ideas

Turning new customer experience ideas into practice isn't always easy. If the CEO asks for something, it is implemented. Most customer experience

Figure 21.3   A prioritization matrix for choosing new customer experience initiatives

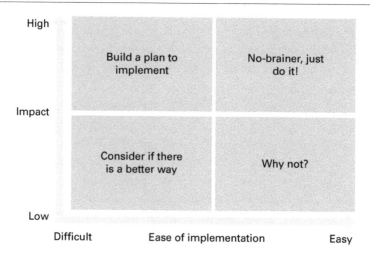

initiatives are not critical and they are seldom the initiative of the CEO. A contributor to the book told us that the enemy of instigating new ideas is good performance at the present.

'We don't have a burning platform here. It's a sort of problem that is under the platform. We are not on fire because we are quite successful. I think CX could be an important addition to our company culture. I'm already having some challenges with top management who think we are doing this already. I think there is a long way to go. The battle has just started.'

All new initiatives need a champion to ensure they are executed. That person needs a certain status within the company and, of equal importance, considerable powers of persuasion to convince everyone that the initiative must happen. They must also be a good planner so that they can make the task look easy by breaking it into its component parts. From there it is a question of bringing together the team of people who will execute the tasks so that all the goals are clear and are understood in terms of who will do what by when. In some companies this champion will be the customer experience manager but where no such person exists it could be task for a marketing or sales manager.

There will be some things that the customer experience team can take charge of and implement. The real measure of a company that has successfully embraced customer experience is one in which others willingly play their part. A simple task, such as sending birthday cards to customers, could be carried out by the CRM team or the account representatives. Setting up an event for customers will need someone to find a venue, someone to arrange speakers and entertainment and someone to invite the customers. Making the arrangements will involve event planners, sales representatives and the marketing team. The more people involved in delivering customer experience throughout the company, the better. It is a sign of a company that has achieved excellent customer experience.

There is a boom in pubs brewing their own beer. Many microbreweries are setting up in pubs in rural areas. Unfortunately, many of the pubs are some distance from mains gas, the preferred fuel for the boilers to produce steam for the brew kettles. This has proved an opportunity for liquid petroleum gas (LPG) suppliers who have tankers that can take gas down remote country lanes. A team in the LPG company had the bright idea of wrapping some of its tankers with a printed vinyl skin that would make them look like huge beer barrels on wheels. They thought that the sight of the jolly beer barrels in the countryside would be a novel customer experience and a great promotion. The story was told to us as a lament because it was so easy to find reasons not to do it. It would have been quite difficult (or at least expensive) to implement and so, as with many initiatives in the north-west corner of the matrix (see Figure 21.1) it sat there as a good idea. It was never fully costed, the impact was never truly assessed and it was never executed. Ideas need champions to make them happen.

Monitoring new initiatives

Throughout the book we have discussed how to measure customer experience. We have seen how to use metrics such as the customer satisfaction score, the Net Promoter Score® and the customer effort score. These quantitative measures show overall levels of satisfaction with customer experience, but they don't provide insights into the new initiatives. A different and more qualitative approach is needed. The customer-facing team should be charged with finding out as much as possible about how new initiatives are received.

- What is it that is liked about the new initiatives?
- Do the initiatives change customer perceptions and if so, in what way?
- Should they be repeated?
- Could they be improved and if so, in what way?
- Will the new initiatives influence the customer to buy more?
- Have certain customers benefited from or enjoyed the initiatives more than others?

It isn't easy but where possible an attempt should be made to establish the return on investment of the new initiative. The aim is to link any new customer experience initiatives with improved results. This will provide a steer for new customer experience initiatives and it will demonstrate to everyone involved in delivering customer experience that it really does work.

Communicating the customer experience results

When something works there should be positive feedback. The successes should be shared and it would be good to alert the leadership team. They are ultimate sponsors of the customer experience initiative and will be eager to know how it is working. The leadership team don't want a 60-page report with all the analytics; they want a summary and if possible on one page.

It is for this reason that the Net Promoter Score® has become so successful. Just like a golf handicap, it is a high-level measure of the customer centricity of the organization. The challenge with metrics of this kind is that they don't change a great deal from one period to another. All the efforts on customer experience and the effect of the new initiatives aren't highlighted in the NPS. Once a high level of customer centricity is reached, the NPS will level off and change little. It is at this stage that anecdotal comment becomes important. The leadership team wants to be assured that the NPS remains high and they need a feel for how the new initiatives are being received. One or two brief stories that illustrate the impact of the initiatives may be all that is required.

Our contributors know that this high-level feedback is vital.

'Over time we have changed the way we think about voice of the customer reporting. We came up with a core of 10 questions and we got a good response. But were we asking the right questions? We had a five-point score instead of a 10-point score. We patted ourselves on the back if we got a high score and thought we didn't need to do anything else. But we weren't gaining as many customers as we expected. When customers left us for a competitor they told us we were not as great as we thought we were. Ticking the "satisfied" box wasn't giving us the insight as to what the customer was feeling. It was cheap to do it that way but it was false economy. Since we have done it properly we've been able to drill down into smaller areas of satisfaction. Before it was just a tick-box exercise.

We were saying that 95 per cent of our customers are satisfied. We've now got a litmus point to say that we made a change here and we can see how satisfaction scores have gone up or down as a result. It is that level of detail that we've now got and not just "Are you satisfied – yes or no?".'

The respect for 'depth' was made by another contributor:

'We report NPS, customer feedback and customer churn internally. We split this in the different product areas in which we operate. NPS we do on an annual basis, the customer churn we do on a weekly basis. We do all the standard logistics things such as deliveries that are OTIF (on time in full) on a daily basis. We do health and safety on a daily basis. We do the customer churn split by which segment the customers are in. We keep it at a high level for the board. They love to hear directly from customers and about two weeks ago a customer was invited as a guest to talk to the EXCOM meeting. We now have regular contact with customers on a more rounded conversation. It isn't just about numbers.'

Our book has discussed every aspect of the customer experience process in business to business companies. After all this discussion we think it is appropriate to give the last word to a contributor that we interviewed who has created one of the best-in-class companies in its field by focusing on customer experience. The starting point for this company is also the end point – well actually not an end point because, as we have said, it is a race that never ends. Throughout the whole of the process – at the start and at the end that never arrives – it is the acknowledgement that we can always do better for our customers. It is getting acceptance that okay isn't good enough. And for this, you really do need to understand your customers:

'Our biggest problem is getting people in our company to realize that they are not doing everything correctly. They have managed and they have done well. You go to one of our territories and they think that everything is okay. They think they don't need all these metrics. The problem is, they're

*not measuring the right things. We've got a balancing act of letting them
see that things could be better. We've got six pillars and I know some other
companies have five and some have four. They are all things for people
to rate themselves on. I couldn't say that culture is the biggest problem or
customer insight or metrics. However, if they've got the customer insight
it puts them in a better shape as they will have a good starting point. We
must never say we have finished. There is always more to do.'*

Things to think about

- How good is your company at constantly improving processes and products to deliver customer experiences that are cheaper, better and faster?
- How good is your company at introducing new delights to customers?
- To what extent do you use complaints to generate ideas for improving customer experience?
- How good is your company at prioritizing new ideas for improved customer experience?
- How good is your company at implementing these new customer experience initiatives?
- How inspiring is the reporting of customer experience performance to people at different levels within your company?

References

Beinhacker, D and Goodman, J (2017) In B2B environments, no news is not good news, *Quirk's* [Online] available from: https://www.quirks.com/articles/in-b2b-environments-no-news-is-not-good-news [last accessed 21 November 2017]

ClearAction (2017) 10 Tips for Customer Experience Innovation [Online] available from: https://clearactioncx.com/10-tips-customer-experience-innovation/ [last accessed 3 October 2017]

Heppell, M (2015) *5 Star Service: How to deliver exceptional customer service*, 3rd edn, Pearson Education, Harlow

Johnson, S (2010) *Where Good Ideas Come From: The natural history of innovation*, Riverhead Books, New York

INDEX

Note: Numbers within main headings, 'Mc' and the symbol '+' are filed as spelt out. Page locators in *italics* denote information contained within a Figure or Table; those in roman numerals denote information within the Preface.